Pleading Your Case

PLEADING YOUR CASE

COMPLAINTS AND RESPONSES

JANET S. KOLE

AMERICAN BAR ASSOCIATION
Defending Liberty
Pursuing Justice

Cover design by ABA Publishing.

Printed in the United States of America.

14 13 12 5 4 3 2

Library of Congress Cataloging-in-Publication Data is on file with the Library of Congress.

ISBN 13: 978-1-61632-829-0

Discounts are available for books ordered in bulk. Special consideration is given to state bars, CLE programs, and other bar-related organizations. Inquire at Book Publishing, ABA Publishing, American Bar Association, 321 North Clark Street, Chicago, Illinois 60654.

www.ShopABA.org

Table of Contents

TEXT BOXES

Acknowledgments

My thanks again to my feisty colleagues, Sherrie Ireland and Nancy Watson, for all their help with this and my previous book, and to the many lawyers who have taught me a thing or two over the years. I will name a few of them only, to save space, but there are others too. So thank you Ira Tiger, Jerry Shestack, Joe Torregrossa, John Lewis, Dennis (the Menace) Brennan, and I miss you, Arthur Littleton, a true gentleman.

And love again and always to my wonderful family, Gabe and Wendy and Susie and Aline.

Introduction: Pleadings

When you think of pleading your client's case, you undoubtedly envision yourself delivering a stirring oral argument in front of a judge or a jury. While that is certainly the endgame in litigation, it is not the beginning. Complaints and answers are called "pleadings" for a reason: they are the initial explanation that you craft as a lawyer to explain your client's position. Although pleadings are written, not oral, they can and should be stirring enough to make your client's position clear.

Pleadings needn't be dry. They can and should convey your fervent belief in your client's cause. While you may not have as much fun pleading in writing as you would orally, you will find the crafting of pleadings intellectually stimulating if you think about the philosophical and historical background of modern day pleading while using the pleadings to tell your client's story.

One of my favorite law professors was a Harvard-educated hard-ass named Joseph H. Koffler. He taught Torts, in a very idiosyncratic way. First, we had to learn about a subspecialty of his—common law pleading. Way back in 1976, when I took his class, as a first year law student at New York Law School, I refused to be intimidated by his bark, which was fierce, but which I discovered later had no bite. The peculiar focus on the subject of common law pleading instead of torts caused me to complain constantly about

"Dry" versus "Wet" Or "Juicy" Pleadings

How is it possible to make pleadings less dry? By thinking outside the box.

One way of both amusing yourself and swaying the judge in your case is to think about some way of referring to your adversary in your complaint or response to the complaint that holds them up to ridicule or sounds like a slur. I don't mean using an epithet, like "slimy predatory defendant," but something more subtle and more persuasive.

For example, when I was a young lawyer, I represented a plaintiff in a commercial dispute against a bank. The majestic sound of the bank's name—we'll call it First Federal Bank of New York—worried the senior partner on the case, who was concerned that the defendant would get the upper hand by naming itself "Federal" for short. So instead, we foreclosed that by using an acronym. The first time we referred to the defendant in the complaint, we called it "defendant First Federal Bank of New York, hereafter 'FFONY.' " The defendant never caught on to what this sounded like when pronounced out loud, and referred to itself throughout the litigation as "FFONY." I suspect it colored the court's view of the parties. Our client won on a motion for summary judgment.

what we were being taught. I used to fight with him in class without fear. For that lack of fear, he nicknamed me "feminist," and would never use my actual name again. "Feminist," he would say, "you can't see it now, but you'll be glad I made you learn this."

He was right.

Common law pleading is now an arcane subject, but every facet of modern legal practice had its beginnings in the common law pleading we inherited from England. Professor Koffler wrote a treatise on the subject, which fascinated him and, because of his teaching, me. Looking back on my many years of practice, I realize how lucky we are today that current legal requirements are more forgiving than they were in the time of our legal system's beginning. A litigant of old was thrown out of court unless his complaint recited certain "magic words" to begin an action. For example, to accuse a wrongdoer of trespassing on your property, you would have to plead that the defendant "with force and arms broke and entered the close of the plaintiff" even where there was, in fact, no "close" or fence, <u>Berger v. Lexington Lumber Co.</u>, 178 S.C. 72, 182 S.E. 156, 157 (S.C. 1935). Failure to use those magic words foreclosed any relief. Today, by contrast, procedural rules spell out that in the interests of justice pleadings should be liberally construed to do justice. The failure to use magic words no longer rings the death knoll for a pleading.

The process of liberalization has proceeded over time; it didn't happen all at once. When I started practicing law in Pennsylvania in 1980, the remnants of common law pleading still existed. A lawyer had to identify in her complaint which of three areas of law was the basis of the first filing. Did the complaint sound in assumpsit (now called "contract"), trespass (now called "tort") or equity? Misidentifying a cause of action could result in having that cause, or even the complaint as a whole, dismissed, usually "without prejudice" (meaning the court would allow you to refile a corrected complaint), but, if the statute of limitations had run, "with prejudice" (meaning you were foreclosed from bringing an action). Today, the Pennsylvania Rules state that there is only one form of action—a civil action—for assumpsit, trespass and equity. Pa. R. Civ. Pro. 1001(b). That's a big change in formalism in a relatively short period of time—less than a generation.

What Is A Dismissal with Prejudice?

If a case is dismissed "with prejudice" it has the same effect as a final judgment on the merits. It begins the running of your time to appeal. It is dispositive of the claims. It has a preclusive effect in other matters involving the same claims.

What Is A Dismissal without Prejudice?

If a case is dismissed "without prejudice" it means that, assuming the statute of limitations has not run, you can refile the action later.

I will leave it to legal philosophers to explain what has caused the shift from strict pleading requirements to the more liberal constructionism of today. But there is no doubt that our legal system has been proceeding toward greater openness and a level playing field for all litigants. The old lawyer's trick of hiding the ball, only to throw it at an opponent on the witness stand for maximum surprise, is now disfavored by rules and by judges. And the magic words are gone, replaced with the sensible requirement that the first court filing—the complaint—state a story in simple language so that the defendant can figure out what the plaintiff is complaining about. (I will discuss later the issue of how much detail in a complaint is required to give the defendant fair notice.) The plain and simple language requirement extends to all pleadings, not just complaints.

For example, N.J.R. Civ. Pro. 4:5-3 says, in pertinent part, "An answer shall state in short and plain terms the pleader's defenses to each claim asserted. . ."

What is a pleading exactly? Most civil procedural rules define pleadings. For example:

> Only these pleadings are allowed: (1) a complaint; (2) an answer to a complaint; (3) an answer to a counterclaim designated as a counterclaim; (4) an answer to a cross-claim; (5) a third-party complaint; (6) an answer to a third-party complaint; and (7) if the court orders one, a reply to answer.

F.R.C.P. 7(a).

At this point in your legal career, even if you have heard of and read complaints and answers, as well as motions to dismiss, you may be in the unenviable position of being asked to draft your first complaint or answer. Where do you begin?

First, and most importantly, read the rules. The rules in your jurisdiction will give you a lot of information—what court you should be in, what needs to be filed as a first filing, whether you need a form cover sheet, whether or not there is a fee for filing, what the timing for answers is, what defenses are available and when they must be made.

What Is A Pleading?

1. Complaint: Written statement, with numbered paragraphs, setting out the story of the plaintiff's case.

2. Answer: Written statement, following numbered paragraphs of complaint, setting out defendant's reply to plaintiff's statement.

Most procedural rules define what a pleading is. For example, F.R.C.P. 7(a) defines the following as pleadings, and allows no others:

(1) a complaint;
(2) an answer to a complaint;
(3) an answer to a counterclaim designated as a counterclaim;
(4) an answer to a crossclaim;
(5) a third-party complaint;
(6) an answer to a third-party complaint; and
(7) if the court orders one, a reply to an answer.

And be sure you read all the rules that apply. Most jurisdictions have general rules and local rules. For example, in Pennsylvania, the state supreme court has promulgated civil procedural rules. Rule 1035 pertains to summary judgment. Each county court, which is a part of the state system, has promulgated its own local rules that modify or expand the requirements of that rule. So, the Montgomery County Court of Common Please has its own version of Rule 1035:

> Rule 1035.2(a). Motion for Summary Judgment.
>
> (1) *Filing.* A motion for summary judgment shall be faced with a cover sheet of the moving party in the form set forth in Local Rule 205.2(b) and shall be accompanied by the moving party's proposed order. The moving party shall check the box on the cover sheet requiring a response, if any, per the Pennsylvania Rules of Civil Procedure. Motions for summary judgment are not given a rule return date by Court Administration.

The same is true in the federal courts; the local district courts have local rules supplementing the federal rules. Read all the rules!

What follows is not meant to be an exhaustive compendium of issues arising in the context of pleadings. Instead, my goal is to alert you to the issues so that you know what you have to think about when crafting a complaint or a response to a complaint. By the way, a response includes a motion as well as an answer.

And don't forget, as I just said, to read the rules. That includes the rules of your local state court, or the federal rules, or the local federal rules. No matter your religion, no matter if you even have a religion, as a lawyer the rules should be your bible.

What A Complaint Looks Like

[THE COURT YOU'RE IN]

In The Court of Common Pleas of Bucks County

[THE CAPTION] **[THE CASE NUMBER]**

Plaintiff Civil Action No: 95-001

v.

Defendant

[THE TITLE OF THE PLEADING]

Complaint

[NUMBERED PARAGRAPHS]

1. The plaintiff, Excellent Person, is a citizen of the Commonwealth of Pennsylvania.
2. The defendant, Dirty Scoundrel, is a citizen of the Commonwealth of Pennsylvania.
3. This case arises out of the breach by Dirty of a contract to build a home for Excellent.
4. This is what happened.

[CAUSES OF ACTION]

Count one—Breach of Contract

xx. Plaintiff repeats here all of the above numbered paragraphs and incorporates them by reference.
xxi. [Elements of the cause of action].
xxii. [How all the elements are met].

[RELIEF YOU WANT, aka ad damnum clause]

Wherefore, plaintiff Excellent demands that. . .

PLEADING YOUR CASE

DRAFTING A COMPLAINT

Part One

Before You Begin

Many of the issues I raise below can be answered by reviewing your local and federal court rules. In some jurisdictions, like New Jersey, the rules come with ample commentary and case citations, to help you hone in on the fine points of procedure. The bottom line is: read the rules as part of your pre-suit research.

A. Making Sense of Your Client's Story

Your client may be highly sophisticated, and be able to narrate her claims in a way that allows you to sit down and write the complaint. Many clients, however, are either unsophisticated or emotional about their claims, or both. In that case, you may find yourself wondering what in the heck it's all about.

In the latter case, you must be an investigator, a psychiatrist and a reporter all rolled into one. A reporter asks "who, what, when, where and why" whenever she writes an article. That's how you should begin with your analysis of your client's story and of your notes.

Who acted against your client (what parties should I sue)?

What did they do (what harm did your client suffer, and are their theories of recovery for that harm)?

When did it happen (is there a statute of limitations problem)?

Where did it happen (where is there jurisdiction, and where is venue proper)?

Why did the defendant act the way he did (are there defenses)?

As the psychiatrist, you must ask yourself if your client has an axe to grind that makes him an unreliable narrator as to the events that occurred. What is the client's current relationship with the prospective defendant? What was the client's past relationship? Has the client sued anyone before? Has the client sued this particular defendant before? Why is the client so emotional?

As an investigator, you will do some of your own digging before preparing the complaint, which includes making your own determination of the facts alleged by your client. Did your client's neighbor really sneak into your client's house to steal his vacuum cleaner? Check to see if your client made a complaint to the police; interview some neighbors. If the allegation seems far-fetched, it's best to leave it out of your complaint.

Even where your client is a corporation, and your contact is the sophisticated general counsel, there may be facts of which he is unaware. If there appear to be holes in the story, or if there are facts you must discover in order to prepare the complaint and satisfy your good faith obligations, you must ask your contact to determine the missing facts and the evidentiary basis for them, or to allow you to review documents and interview employees before you draft the complaint.

B. Causes of Action

1. What Are Your Client's Causes of Action?

In general, a plaintiff can only recover for a wrong where the common law or a statute spells out the relief to which he is entitled because of that wrong. As you probably remember from law school, the theory of recovery for this wrong is known as a cause of action. Generally, a cause of action arises out of a tort or out of a contract. Statutory causes of action are based on policy decisions of the legislature that certain injuries demand redress.

You must figure out, after interviewing your client, what harm your client has suffered. Then you must determine whether or not there is a cause of action for that harm. It may remind you of a law school exam or even, horrors, the bar exam. ("How many causes of action can you find in this factual scenario?") You may have some good ideas about the causes of action, but you should not proceed to draft a complaint until you have done research on the injury and its potential remedies. Every state has its own statutes, and so does the federal government, and these as well as common law provide a plaintiff with causes as well as remedies.

If the plaintiff was injured in an automobile accident, for example, he can sue the driver who caused the accident for negligence. Negligence is a cause of action. It "sounds" in tort. Or the plaintiff might sue the manufacturer of his own car when the brakes failed and caused an accident, on the ground that the brakes were negligently made. Or the plaintiff might sue his car dealer for faulty repair of his brakes. This, too, is negligence.

Where automobiles are concerned, however, many states also have a statutory right to relief for so-called "lemons"—cars that have never worked right and that break down even after repeated repairs. These statutes are called "lemon laws," and provide a different cause of action from negligence. Lemon laws are a hybrid of negligence and contract breach in terms of a cause of action.

Some jurisdictions have statutory remedies that are unique. In Louisiana, to name an outlying example, a product defect suit where the consumer has warned the manufacturer of a problem that has not been solved is a cause of action for "redhibition." Without research, or unless you want to law school at Tulane, you will never have heard of this cause of action.

Again, the key to determining what causes of action your client has is research.

2. What Are The Elements of The Cause of Action?

Cast your mind back to law school. What are the elements of the tort of negligence? Generally, the defendant has (1) a duty to the plaintiff; and (2) defendant breached the duty; and (3) the breach caused an (4) injury to plaintiff.

When you are researching what causes of action your client has, you must ensure that the allegations of your complaint set out the elements and that the facts match the allegations. Did the defendant owe a duty to your client? If not, without some state law exception that I won't go into here, you cannot make out a cause of action for negligence.

The failure to allege sufficient facts to support all the elements of a cause of action will enable a defendant to seek dismissal on the ground of failure to state a claim. You must be familiar with the elements of any cause of action you plead. The elements of common law causes of action, whether tort or contract, are set out in caselaw in your jurisdiction. It is imperative that you research what the elements are, and that you don't rely on your law school or bar exam memory. Each jurisdiction has its own nuances for even seemingly simple and familiar causes. For example, in Pennsylvania the courts set out four elements for the tort of negligence—duty, breach, causation and injury—while in some states and in the Restatement of Torts, there is a fifth element, "proximate cause." Without getting into either his-

What Is A Cause of Action?

When a plaintiff suffers an injury, the wrong that has caused the injury is a "cause of action." A cause can sound in negligence or contract, or can derive from a statute.

tory or caselaw, let me quickly remind you what proximate cause is ("proximate" has the same root as "proximity"). It means that the defendant's breach of duty was closely, not remotely, related to the harm that plaintiff suffered.

Whether you are in a four element or five element jurisdiction, it is important that you find out what the elements are for your cause of action and that you allege facts to support each of them in the complaint. This obviously is true for every cause of action, whether based in tort, contract or statute.

3. What Is The Statute of Limitations?

At the very beginning of your research into causes of action you should check the statute of limitations for each cause. Perhaps you only have a day to file. Perhaps your client is out of time. Perhaps the time hasn't even begun to run yet. Whatever the outcome of this research, though, be sure to convey the news to your client. If you find that your client has consulted you after the statute has run on the causes of action, put that fact in writing. Being kicked out of court on statute of limitations grounds is humiliating. Even worse is being sued for malpractice.

4. Does Your Client Have Standing?

We all learned about standing in law school. Few of us know how to explain it to non-lawyers. Here is the Supremes view of it: "In essence the question of standing is whether the litigant is entitled to have the court decide the merits of the dispute or of particular issues." Warth v. Seldin, 422 U.S. 490, 498 (1975).

So now that you have figured out what causes of action your client may have, you must also determine if your client has standing to sue. In most instances, it will be obvious. For example, your client was injured in an auto accident while a passenger. There is no doubt that she has standing to sue for her injuries.

A more difficult case is presented where, for example, a citizens group, like the Sierra Club, seeks to enforce environmental laws against some alleged polluter. The Sierra Club is not obviously directly "injured" by the pollution. In such a situation, you will need to find either reported cases in your jurisdiction like the one you seek to bring or statutes or implementing regulations that grant standing to your plaintiff. In some jurisdictions, there are statutes that grant standing to private parties acting for the good of the public to bring a lawsuit seeking to right a wrong, even if the plaintiff cannot show a direct injury. For example, in New Jersey, the Environmental Rights Act grants standing to citizens groups to sue for violation of any environmental statute in the state that would otherwise not provide a right to sue. Although the concept of standing is related to whether or not your client can bring his case to court, it is not the same as jurisdiction, which I discuss below. It is more properly understood as whether your client has a right to relief.

C. What Relief Do You Want?

Wasn't it Freud who asked "What do women want?" Had he been a lawyer instead of a psychiatrist, he would have said: "What do clients want, for heaven's sake?"

Are There Pre-Suit Requirements?

Whether your cause of action is based on the common law or on a statute, be sure before you file a complaint that you have followed the pre-suit requirements of the common law cause of action or of the statute. For example, if you intend to bring a lawsuit under the federal Resource Conservation and Recovery Act ("RCRA") to require a landowner, operator or polluter to clean up contamination at a site, you must first give the defendant (and the president of the United States, the Environmental Protection Agency ("EPA") and your state environmental agency, among others) 60 days notice before you do so, in order to give the defendant the opportunity to voluntarily remedy the violation of RCRA and/or to give the EPA or the state agency the opportunity to jump in to order the remedy. Failure to give 60 days notice is fatal to the complaint, which will be dismissed. See Hallstrom v. Tillamook, 493 U.S. 20 (1989).

Not only must you be sure you know what remedy your client wants and which remedy she is entitled to. You must also be sure that the statute of limitations for the remedy you seek, which is linked to your cause of action, hasn't run out. For example, in New York, in an action for breach of fiduciary duty a plaintiff can seek damages or an injunction. The two remedies have different limitations periods: money damages must be sought within three years while equitable relief can be sought within six years. If the three year limitations period has already run, you will want to craft a complaint that requires equitable relief.[1]

1. Remedies for Your Causes of Action

What does your client want from this lawsuit? Sometimes when you ask your client that, you'll hear, as I have on occasion, it's "justice." But most of the time, it's something much more tangible, like money. You can't craft a complaint until you know what your client is seeking from the defendant.

Causes of action have to be matched to the relief they provide. An example is a statutory claim where the only relief under the statute is injunctive. You can't ask for money damages where the statute doesn't provide for it.

Remedies

1. Money damages:
   - compensate for harm
   - money owed under a contract
   - restitution
   - unjust enrichment
2. Equitable remedies:
   - injunctions—prohibitory
   - injunctions—mandatory
   - specific performance
3. Sanctions.
4. Punitive damages.
5. Attorneys' fees.
6. Penalties.
7. Declaratory judgment.

---

[1] IDT Corp. v. Morgan Stanley Dean Witter & Co., --N.Y.3d--, (Ct. App., First Dept. 2009).

Legal scholars have written treatises on remedies. Generally speaking, relief boils down to money damages or equitable remedies. The latter include prohibitory as well as mandatory injunctions (either stopping someone from acting a certain way or forcing them to do something). Although all claims for relief and causes of action can all be brought in one action in most jurisdictions, it is wise to check your rules to be sure you don't have to bring your equitable claims in a court of chancery, an orphan's court, a "special part," or a surrogate's court.

2. Your Client's Right to The Relief S/he Seeks

The inquiry you must make when thinking about your client's right to relief is similar but not identical to the question of standing. For example, your client may have a right to injunctive relief only, not money damages. The Resource Conservation and Recovery Act (RCRA), 42 U.S.C. §6901 et seq., provides that a party who has violated RCRA's provisions regarding handling of hazardous substances can be forced to remedy the harm—i.e., a plaintiff can seek injunctive relief under the Act. There is, however, no right under RCRA for a plaintiff who has been forced to spend money on cleaning up a defendant's contamination to recover its costs of cleanup from the defendant. To recover the past cleanup costs, the plaintiff must look to some other cause of action, either at common law or pursuant to a statute.

D. The Proper Venue

What court must you be in? And if you have a choice of courts, which of them do you want to be in?

1. What Court Is Proper?

"Venue" is both a legal term of art and a common noun. In both cases, it means "place."

Whether you file your action in the right "place" depends on a number of factors. First, of course, look at the rules. Civil procedural rules will tell you where venue is "laid"—i.e., if you're in the right court. The New Jersey state rules are typical in this regard:

> . . . venue . . . shall be laid in the county in which the cause of action arose, or in which any party to the action resides at the time of commencement, or in which the summons was served on a nonresident defendant. . .

N.J.R. Civ. Pro. 4:3-2(a).

Sometimes, the proper "place" for filing will be found in a statute, not in court rules. In federal court, for example, 28 USC Section 1391 controls venue:

> **(a)** A civil action wherein jurisdiction is founded only on diversity of citizenship may, except as otherwise provided by law, be brought only in
>
> **(1)** a judicial district where any defendant resides, if all defendants reside in the same State,
>
> **(2)** a judicial district in which a substantial part of the events or omissions giving rise to the claim occurred, or a substantial part of property that is the subject of the action is situated, or
>
> **(3)** a judicial district in which any defendant is subject to personal jurisdiction at the time the

action is commenced, if there is no district in which the action may otherwise be brought.

(b) A civil action wherein jurisdiction is not founded solely on diversity of citizenship may, except as otherwise provided by law, be brought only in

(1) a judicial district where any defendant resides, if all defendants reside in the same State,

(2) a judicial district in which a substantial part of the events or omissions giving rise to the claim occurred, or a substantial part of property that is the subject of the action is situated, or

(3) a judicial district in which any defendant may be found, if there is no district in which the action may otherwise be brought.

The statute goes on to provide for specific situations that might arise (including where you can sue a corporation or a state), but this gives you an idea that proper venue is defined either by a court rule or a statute.

Notice that the federal venue statute requires jurisdiction as a predicate to suit. I will discuss jurisdiction below.

2. What Court Do You Want to Be In?

Let's say venue would be proper in either your local federal district court or your state court. And let's assume for purposes of this discussion that jurisdiction will exist in either court. (Again, more below.) Which is better for your client?

In Philadelphia, Pennsylvania, where I have practiced for many years, the mantra of all local lawyers is that if you're a plaintiff in a personal injury case, you want to be in the local county court—the Philadelphia Court of Common Pleas—because Philadelphia juries are more likely to award damages, and significant ones at that, to plaintiffs. By contrast, if your plaintiff is a corporation suing another corporation, you want to be in federal court because the judges and juries are more sophisticated and will understand the nuances of a commercial dispute.

This is, of course, a gross simplification. Nevertheless, you should talk to more experienced lawyers about the reputation of each court for sympathy to your kind of case. This should factor into your decision as to where to file your complaint.

Another important consideration is the speed of justice. Does the docket move faster in federal court? Or is there a local court with a "rocket docket?" Usually, the plaintiff wants speedy justice, and this should also factor in to your decision.

Of course, you may not have a choice. This is where "jurisdiction" rears its head.

E. Jurisdiction

You probably remember from your civil procedure course in law school that there are two kinds of jurisdiction. There is subject matter jurisdiction, without which a court cannot hear your client's case. And there is personal jurisdiction, without which you cannot reach the defendant to obtain relief for your client.

1. Subject Matter Jurisdiction

What courts—state, federal, municipal—have subject matter jurisdiction in your case? You will look to statutes, rules and your local (state) constitution to determine the answer.

The legislators of each state determine by statute, or the voters determine through constitutional provisions, the subject matter jurisdiction of each of the state's courts. In the federal courts, the United States Constitution, Article III, Section 2, grants limited subject matter jurisdiction to the federal courts, and federal statutes elucidate the details of what the federal courts can hear.

I will use the federal example because it applies everywhere in the country. But you must do your own research about the court you want to be in.

The statutory guides for the federal courts are found in Title 28 of the U.S. Code. Section 1331 provides for so-called "federal question" jurisdiction: "The district courts shall have original jurisdiction of all civil actions arising under the Constitution, laws, or treaties of the United States." Section 1332 provides for subject matter jurisdiction where there is diversity of citizenship among the parties, and where the threshold amount at issue is high enough.

> **(a)** The district courts shall have original jurisdiction of all civil actions where the matter in controversy exceeds the sum or value of $75,000, exclusive of interest and costs, and is between—
>
> **(1)** citizens of different States;
>
> **(2)** citizens of a State and citizens or subjects of a foreign state;

(3) citizens of different States and in which citizens or subjects of a foreign state are additional parties; and

(4) a foreign state, defined in section 1603(a) of this title, as plaintiff and citizens of a State or of different States.

State versus Federal: The Issues

If you are challenged about your choice of jurisdiction (i.e., federal court versus state court), and are forced to write a brief on the subject, you should be aware of the issues that can arise in these situations.

1. Removal and remand: a defendant may remove a case begun in state court to federal court, and a plaintiff may challenge the removal and insist the federal court remand to state court.
2. Supplemental jurisdiction: if the plaintiff has brought a statutory claim where a particular court is designated as the only appropriate forum, other non-statutory claims that are sufficiently related to the statutory claim may be heard by the designated court even where these other claims do not have an independent jurisdictional basis to be in the designated court. See U.S.C. Section 1367.
3. Abstention: a court designated by statute to hear a claim may abstain from hearing additional non-statutory claims. Also, where two separate actions are pending in two different courts, one may abstain from hearing the matter while it is pending in the other court.

Similarly, Article 6 of the New Jersey Constitution creates the state courts. However, unlike the federal courts, which are of limited jurisdiction, the New Jersey courts are courts of general jurisdiction.

Make sure you file your complaint in a court with subject matter jurisdiction. This kind of jurisdiction cannot be manufactured or simply agreed to by the parties, and lack of subject matter jurisdiction cannot be waived. There is nothing worse than finding out, after endless litigation and a trial, that the court never had subject matter jurisdiction over your case, and the entire effort is a nullity.

By contrast, a plaintiff's lack of standing can be waived.

a. Judicial Prejudice

As an important aside, remember that judges are human (although you may not always think so). As a result, your case may run afoul of a judge's personal prejudice, politics or pet peeve. Some judges have been known to dismiss cases on a purported lack of jurisdiction ground even where other judges have taken the identical case without a peep. See any number of federal circuit court conflicts as examples. (Here's one: the right to seek enforcement of a settlement agreement after dismissal of the case on the record. The Seventh Circuit says: ok. The Third Circuit says: you're out of court because there's no subject matter jurisdiction. See Ford v. Neese, 119 F.3d. 560 (7th Cir. 1997), and Shaffer v. GTE N., Inc., 284 F.3d 500 (3rd Cir. 2002).)

Some jurists may bar the courthouse door to cases they hate by claiming the plaintiff has no standing to bring the

Service of Process and Personal Jurisdiction

The term of art, "service of process," means making sure the defendant has received proper notice of the lawsuit and has received a copy of the complaint. Every jurisdiction has its own rules for proper service. In some states, process can only be served by people over 18. In some states, you must serve the complaint directly to the defendant. In some states, you can leave the complaint for the defendant at his regular place of business or his domicile. The means of achieving proper service are many.

But the most important thing to remember is that even if you properly serve the complaint, if the defendant is not subject to personal jurisdiction, you've wasted both your client's money and your time. The only exception is where the defendant has waived personal jurisdiction, either by agreement or by entering an appearance and failing to raise lack of personal jurisdiction.

If you are lucky enough to be practicing in a law firm, there are three classes of people who can help you achieve service of process: litigation secretaries, paralegals, and other lawyers. Use all these resources. If you are practicing on your own, be sure to ask other lawyers how to serve process; you can even ask your court clerk how to do it.

claim. Or they may place the date that the statute of limitations begins to run well before most plaintiffs could possibly react.

With all of your best efforts, you may not be able to anticipate every jurisdictional hurdle, possibility or problem. When you draw a judge who has a personal agenda that manifests itself as a jurisdictional or jurisprudential dispute, be prepared to warn your client that the case has just become much more complicated and will, consequently, be much more expensive to litigate.

But there is balance in the world. Sometimes a judge wants to give the plaintiff a forum, even where caselaw exists which could put the plaintiff out of court. That is presumably why the Seventh Circuit said the district court, in the Ford v. Neese case above, had jurisdiction to enforce the settlement, despite the Supreme Court's opinion in Kokkonen v. Guardian Life Ins., 511 U.S. 375 (1994), holding that there must be an independent ground for subject matter jurisdiction to enforce a settlement agreement.

Because these real world happenings can't be anticipated by anyone, you should be sure to tell your client before you file your complaint that absolutely anything can happen. That's why I never give my client an estimate of our chances of winning that are any higher than fifty-fifty.

2. Personal Jurisdiction

Is it fair to bring the defendant in your case into the court you've chosen? Each jurisdiction has its own rules for personal jurisdiction. Generally speaking, these rules are found under the rubric of "long-arm jurisdiction." In other words, can the long arm of the law reach out to touch the defen-

Jurisdiction versus Standing

Some lawyers—and some judges, too—mix up the concepts of subject matter jurisdiction and standing. Here is an excellent appellate decision that explains the difference, and clarifies that some lower court judges have been getting it wrong.

> It is well-settled that issues relating to subject matter jurisdiction may be raised at any time. . .
>
> Subject matter jurisdiction refers to the court's power to hear and determine cases of the general class to which the proceedings in questions belong. . .
>
> We have previously indicated that a party's lack of standing as a real party in interest deprives a court of subject matter jurisdiction. . .
>
> However, the wealth of authority is to the effect that the issue of a party's status as real party in interest does not involve subject matter jurisdiction.
>
> The purpose of a real party in interest provision is to assure that a defendant is required only to defend an action brought by a proper party and that such an action need be defended only once. 59AmJur2d *Parties* §35 (1987). The right of a plaintiff to maintain a suit, while frequently treated as going to the question of jurisdiction, goes, in reality, to the right of the plaintiff to relief rather than to the jurisdiction of the court to afford it. . .
>
> We hold the issue of whether a party is a "real party in interest" does not involve subject matter jurisdiction. To the extent previous caselaw has indicated to the contrary, it is overruled.

Bardoon Properties v. Eidolon Corp., --S.E.2d--, (S.C.S.Ct. 1997) dant and haul his butt into court? Most states rules provide that state long-arm jurisdiction is as broad as federal jurisprudence allows under the U.S. Constitution.

The U.S. Supreme Court and numerous district and state courts have opined on what activities or attributes subject a defendant to the personal jurisdiction of a court. Without repeating here the many long discussions by the courts, let me give a few "sound bites" that will give you a sense of the issues you must think about to be sure you can obtain personal jurisdiction over the defendant.

- "Minimum contacts"—has the defendant purposely acted within the state to which you seek to bring him to defend the lawsuit?
- "Substantial acts"—have the defendant's acts within the state been substantial?
- "Notions of fundamental fairness"—are the contacts substantial enough so that hauling the defendant into court is fair?
- "Due process"—is the defendant receiving actual notice of the claims against her, and does she have an opportunity to be heard?

Unlike subject matter jurisdiction, lack of personal jurisdiction can be waived, either by contract or by the defendant's activities in the litigation, i.e., failing to raise lack of personal jurisdiction as a defense, and defending on the merits.

If you don't have personal jurisdiction over the defendant, you may serve the complaint pursuant to local rules,

Jurisdictional Analysis

The wise lawyer will always include jurisdictional analysis in case preparation.

What court do I want to be in? Although it is mainly plaintiffs who can make this choice, the federal removal statute on occasion puts this issue into play for defendants as well. Forum non conveniens (inconvenient forum) arguments also can be made by defendants to give themselves a degree of choice.

Assuming you have a choice between state and federal courts (or even among different states) and neither lack of venue nor jurisdiction prevent you from choosing a hospitable court, forum shop. Find out what court has the best law on your subject matter. If, for example, you are a plaintiffs' class action lawyer, it helps to know that the judges you may draw in a particular circuit generally are conservative, dislike class actions, and hate plaintiffs' lawyers. You would then avoid that venue at all costs.

Sometimes, however, the choice of forum is not yours to make.

but service will be a nullity if the defendant raises the issue and wins. Be sure you have personal jurisdiction and that you can serve the defendant under your local rules. In New Jersey, for example, Rule 4:4-4 spells out both how a defendant can be served and whether a defendant is amenable to service in the first place.

Writing The Complaint

My writing background is that of a feature news reporter. When I wrote feature articles, my goal was to create a story that a reader would want to read to the end.

Believe it or not, you want to do the same with a complaint. The story you want to tell should be the compelling version of how your client was injured by the dastardly defendant. But wait, you say. What about all those pesky recitals you have to make at the beginning of a complaint, such as identifying the parties, setting out the jurisdictional basis of your complaint, and reciting that venue is properly laid?

Well, yes, you still have to include some technical requirements. But THEN you can tell a story.

A. The "Boilerplate"

Each jurisdiction has its own requirements for what every complaint must contain at a minimum. As always, look at the rules to determine what the requirements are. Rule 8(a)(1) of the Federal Rules of Civil Procedure, for example, says:

> "(a) Claim for Relief. A pleading that states a claim for relief must contain:
>
> (1) a short and plain statement of the grounds for the court's jurisdiction, unless the court already has jurisdiction and the claim needs no new jurisdictional support . . ."

By contrast, New Jersey Rule of Civil Procedure 4:5-2, which sets out the requirements for a complaint, makes no mention of jurisdiction as a necessary element of the first pleading. A New Jersey plaintiff in state court is not required to assert that jurisdiction is proper. As always, check the rules in your court.

The Federal Rules helpfully include the language required to be used in a complaint to assert jurisdiction in Form 7 of the Appendix of Forms:

a. (*For diversity-of-citizenship jurisdiction.*) The plaintiff is [a citizen of *Michigan*] [a corporation incorporated under the laws of *Michigan* with its principal place of business in *Michigan*]. The defendant is [a citizen of *New York*] [a corporation incorporated under the laws of *New York* with its principal place of business in *New York*]. The amount in controversy, without interest and costs, exceeds the sum or value specified by 28 U.S.C. § 1332.

b. (*For federal-question jurisdiction.*) This action rises under [the United States

Constitution, *specify the article or amendment and the section*] [a United States treaty *specify*] [a federal statute, __ U.S.C. § ___].

c. (*For a claim in the admiralty or maritime jurisdiction.*) This is a case of admiralty or maritime jurisdiction. (*To invoke admiralty status under Rule 9(h) use the following:* This is an admiralty or maritime claim within the meaning of Rule 9(h).)

If you are in a state court like New Jersey's you can forget about this boilerplate. But if your court rules require some other boilerplate, be sure to insert it.

B. The Parties

It is after you have gotten through the boilerplate that your creativity can begin to flow. For example, you will want to identify the parties to the complaint in such a way that the plaintiff comes across as noble and wronged, and the defendant as a scheming miscreant. Most complaints identify the parties dryly at the beginning, and continue to do so throughout the body of the complaint. So, you will often see: "Defendant, XYZ Corporation (hereafter referred to as "corporation"). . ."

You don't want to do this dry, factual designation. Instead, you want to subtly start the judge or the judge's law clerk thinking badly of the defendant. Of course, you want to do this judiciously. Do not say: "Defendant, hereinafter called 'dirty rotten bastard' . . ." You can get your point across using equally evocative language with a little thought.

For example, as I mentioned above, "First Federal Bank of New York," your defendant, could be referred to as "FFONY." The acronym is pronounced as if it is the word "phony." The advantage to plotting this out at the time you write your complaint is that forever during the lawsuit, your nemesis will be known as "phony," and all the attributes of that name will be unconsciously attributed to the defendant.

You must do the same with the plaintiff's name. You will not always be lucky enough to have as your client "The Church of Saints," which you could plausibly call "Saints" throughout the complaint. But at the very least, you should be able to name your plaintiff in a way that is inoffensive.

But what, you ask, should you do if the plaintiff is the Bank? You certainly don't want to give the defense naming rights in the answer. You must get ahead of the game by finding a name that is inoffensive and that takes the wind out of the defense's sails. For example, "First Federal" has a nice ring to it; it is very patriotic. And if you're in New York state court, you might prefer to be called "New York."

Sometimes, of course, you'll luck out and your opponent's name won't need any tweaking. Real last names that I'm aware of include Putz, Schmuck and Dick. While the owners of these names undoubtedly have family pride in them, they are fraught with baggage for most of us. (Of course, you could luck out and have a Mensch for a client.) Some names just sound bad; as the jelly commercial says, "with a name like Smucker's, we've got to be good."

If you are the lawyer representing the party with the unfortunate name, you can avoid using the last name and instead use the first. Instead of "Plaintiff Putz," say "Plaintiff Sarah," which has the additional benefit of humanizing her. I don't purport to have the be-all and end-all for the treatment of names, so please don't write or call me for suggestions. My point is that you can be creative and effective as an advocate by thinking outside the box.

C. The Facts

Although preparing a complaint requires that you use the regulated format of numbered paragraphs, there is no rule that your story of how the defendant harmed the plaintiff be stilted. The same thought that goes into "shaping" your case and crafting a story for the judge or jury should go into the recitation of facts in the complaint. Really, you're writing a novel. Ignore those pesky numbers you have to insert.

I always draft the Facts portion of a complaint by writing it first as if it were a short story or feature article in a newspaper. When I was a reporter, I learned the "five Ws": every news article should have right up front the who, what, when, where and why of the story. It should be the same with your complaint. And by focusing on the Ws, you can explain quickly and clearly to the judge and/or clerk why your client is in court and what relief the judge can grant, without extraneous and time-consuming facts. You do <u>not</u> want the reader to wonder: why is this lawyer telling me this?

A good storyteller doesn't get bogged down in details. On the other hand, in certain circumstances, caselaw or a statute may force you to insert details that you wouldn't necessarily include if you were telling your spouse a story. For the most part, the difference is between notice pleading and fact pleading.

As I mentioned in the introduction, the tendency of the federal rules over the years has been toward liberalization of pleading requirements; Rule 8 only requires of the pleader "a short and plain statement of the claim showing that the pleader is entitled to relief. . ." F.R.C.P. 8(A)(2). The Supreme Court interpreted this, in Conley v. Gibson, 355 U.S. 41 (1957), to require a plaintiff only to give a defendant fair notice of the claim. If a judge could imagine any set of circumstances under which the plaintiff had a cause of action, based on the allegations of the complaint, the plaintiff would not be subject to dismissal. This is also the case in many states were "notice pleading" is the rule.

In 2007 and 2009, the U.S. Supreme Court overturned fifty years of precedent with a pair of cases, Bell Atlantic v. Twombly, 554 U.S. 544 (2007), and Ashcroft v. Iqbal, 129 S. Ct. 1937 (2009), that heightened the pleading standard in federal cases. While many practitioners were *shocked* about the change, many lawyers practice in states where fact pleading is a way of life, and for them, the change makes little difference to their legal lives. For example, Pennsylvania is a fact pleading state. Pennsylvania lawyers will have no problems with the legacy of Twombly and Iqbal.

The Pennsylvania Rules of Civil Procedure provide a good guide for drafters of a complaint in a fact-pleading jurisdiction.

Rule 1019. Contents of Pleadings. General and Specific Averments.

(a) The material facts on which a cause of action or defense is based shall be stated in a concise and summary form.

(b) Averments of fraud or mistake shall be averred with particularity. Malice, intent, knowledge, and other conditions of mind may be averred generally.

(c) In pleading the performance or occurrence of conditions precedent, it is sufficient to aver generally that all conditions precedent have been performed or have occurred. A denial of such performance or occurrence shall be made specifically and with particularity.

(d) In pleading an official document or official act, it is sufficient to identify it by reference and aver that the document was issued or the act done in compliance with law.

(e) In pleading a judgment, order or decision of a domestic or foreign court, judicial or administrative tribunal, or board, commission or officer, it is sufficient to aver the judgment, order or decision without setting forth matter showing jurisdiction to render it.

(f) Averments of time, place and items of special damage shall be specifically stated.

(g) Any part of a pleading may be incorporated by reference in another part of the same pleading or in another pleading in the same action. A party may incorporate by reference any matter of record in any State or Federal court of record whose records are within the county in which the action is pending, or any matter which is recorded or transcribed verbatim in the office of the prothonotary, clerk of any court of record, recorder of deeds or register of wills of such county.

(h) When any claim or defense is based upon an agreement, the pleading shall state specifically if the agreement is oral or written.

Official Note:

If the agreement is in writing, it must be attached to the pleading. See subdivision (i) of this rule.

(i) When any claim or defense is based upon a writing, the pleader shall attach a copy of the writing, or the material part thereof, but if the writing or copy is not accessible to the pleader, it is sufficient so to state, together with the reason, and to set forth the substance of the writing.

Pa. R. Civ. Pro. 1019.

Because the Pennsylvania rule requires a recitation of material facts, not just a "short and plain statement of the claim," it is a fact pleading state.

You must determine if the jurisdiction you're in is a notice pleading or fact pleading one. And you also must determine what that means to the courts in that jurisdiction. Just as the U.S. Supreme Court has imposed new requirements that bring federal civil procedure closer to a fact pleading jurisdiction than it was before Twombly, the highest court of your jurisdiction may have shaped or modified what the civil procedural rules say. Do your homework.

Many commentators have written articles and spoken at CLE programs on the changes wrought by Twombly and Iqbal. I can't hope to replicate the points they make here, and that isn't the focus of this book. You must determine for yourself what the pleading standard is in your jurisdiction, and ensure that you can resist a motion to dismiss when you draft your complaint.

D. The Counts

As I mentioned earlier in this book, you will by now have determined what causes of action exist against the defendant. In a complaint, each cause of action is set out as a separate "count." In some jurisdictions, each count is identified by the cause of action as well as the sequential number of the count, as in:

1. Count IV—Negligence

In some jurisdictions, the common practice is to number the counts but not to identify the cause of action. I believe the better practice is to identify the cause of action that the count contains. If your opponent files a motion to dismiss, for example, and a judge agrees as to some but not all of the arguments, you may receive an order that reads something like:

> As to defendant's motion to dismiss counts 1-7 of the complaint, the motion is DENIED except as to count 4, which is hereby DISMISSED.

Your life, as well as that of the judge, will be much easier if you have labeled your counts, so that you can consult your complaint and on its face determine that your cause of action for emotional distress was stricken, but all of your other claims have survived.

A Word About Twombly and Iqbal— Or Any Caselaw

The United States Supreme Court's ruling in any case, Twombly included, is precedent only as long as it's precedent. In other words, even the Supremes change their minds, and you shouldn't rely on your memory or this book to tell you what the law is. How far you have to go to adequately describe your case is a matter you must research, and you must check each time you draft a complaint to be sure the case you relied upon is still good law. After all, Twombly changed 50 years of precedent in the instant it was issued by the Supreme Court. And any precedent can be rendered irrelevant by later legislation. So check before you assume you know the state of the law.

The numbering of counts does not excuse your continuing duty to number the paragraphs sequentially. While this may seem obvious, the peculiarity of pleading everywhere in this country includes a "repetition" paragraph at the beginning of every count which realleges every fact you've plead in the complaint and incorporates it into the count.

"What does she mean?" I hear you say. It's like this: at the beginning of every count, your first numbered paragraph will say: "Plaintiff realleges here paragraphs 1 through [last numbered paragraph] of the complaint as if fully set forth, and incorporates them herein by reference."

Why do you do this? Blame our heritage of common law pleading. In addition to the "magic words" that used to be required, each and every fact on which plaintiff relies has to be incorporated into every count, even though plaintiff has already recited it. The fiction is that each count stands alone, and that the court needs to see which facts apply to which cause of action. The reality is that a bare repetition such as the above is not the same as actually reciting the relevant facts again, but this shorthand reference to the facts as a whole seems to satisfy the atavistic need to have each count be self-sufficient.

Many jurisdictions specifically provide for this repetition and incorporation by reference. For example, in New Jersey, the rules provide in relevant part:

> Statements in a pleading and exhibits to a
> pleading may be adopted by reference in a

> different part of the same pleading or in another pleading or in any motion.

N.J.R. Civ. Pro. 1:4-3.

However, in some jurisdictions with heightened pleading standards, you may find that you have to recite specific facts again in each count to support that particular count, even though you have incorporated by reference. "Plaintiffs are reminded that they must state which factual allegations are supportive of each count." McNeil v. Alternative Home Financing, Inc., No. 2:04-cv-356-FTM-33DNF, (M.D. Fl 2006) (granting plaintiffs leave to amend their complaint).

E. The Wherefore Clause

Years ago, and probably still in some jurisdictions, the part of the complaint where you asked for relief was called the "ad damnum" clause. It is now more commonly known as the "Wherefore" clause, for the simple reason that the request for relief begins with the capitalized word "Wherefore."

Local practice differs, though. In some jurisdictions, you will append a Wherefore clause at the end of each count. In others, the Wherefore comes at the very end of the complaint. How you phrase your request is also a matter of local practice. In some jurisdictions, you can get away with reciting something simple, such as:

> "WHEREFORE, plaintiff demands judgment in its favor as to all the relief to which it is entitled."

In other jurisdictions, you must set out each element of the relief you seek:

> "WHEREFORE, plaintiff demands judgment in its favor on counts 1 through 4 of the complaint, and an immediate injunction forbidding defendant from continuing to defame plaintiff, plus damages for emotional distress in an amount in excess of [jurisdictional amount to get into court], plus such other relief as the court deems just and proper."

Do you want attorneys' fees? (Of course, your client does, but is your client entitled to them under a statute or caselaw?) Do you want costs (different from attorneys' fees—usually filing fees and possibly costs of service of process)? It's always a good idea to add a request for fees and costs to the Wherefore paragraph.

So, as always, read the rules and try to find a template from your colleagues that will give you the keys to local practice in your jurisdiction.

F. Miscellaneous Considerations

1. Verification

Must your complaint be verified? For some causes of action in some jurisdictions, you must append a signed verification from the plaintiff attesting to the truthfulness of the allegations of the complaint. In some jurisdictions, such as Pennsylvania, every complaint must be verified. In federal court, no verification of the complaint is required except for certain claims. Check the rules! And, as a prudential matter, don't verify the pleading yourself. If your client has scammed you, and you have attested to the veracity of the untrue allegations, you can be in deep trouble with your state bar as well as with your bosses and the judges in your jurisdiction.

2. Jury Trial

Do you want a jury trial? In many jurisdictions, if you don't request a jury trial in the complaint, you can't ask for it later. In some jurisdictions, such as Pennsylvania, you must make the jury demand on the face of the complaint. In others, such as New Jersey, a jury demand is pleaded in a separate section at the end of the complaint, along with a statement of the identity of trial counsel. If you think you might want a jury trial, the best practice is to ask for it. If as the case proceeds you change your mind, in most jurisdictions you can waive the jury demand.

3. Other Local Requirements

Are there other requirements for the complaint in your jurisdiction? In some states, such as New Jersey, and in the federal courts, you must file with the complaint a case information statement that allows the clerk to determine whether the case is complex and requires minimal or maximal discovery. In some jurisdictions today, you must file a notice in both English and Spanish notifying the defendant that "you have been sued." In Pennsylvania, you must stamp a "notice to defend" on the complaint with the due date of the response.

So:

Rule 1018.1. Notice to Defend. Form.

(a) Every complaint filed by a plaintiff and every complaint filed by a defendant against an additional defendant shall begin with a notice to defend in substantially the form set forth in subdivision (b). No other notice to plead to a complaint shall be required.

(b)

[CAPTION]

Notice

You have been sued in court. If you wish to defend against the claims set forth in the following pages, you must take action within twenty (20) days after this complaint and notice are served, by entering a written appearance personally or by attorney and filing in writing with the court your defenses or objections to the claims set forth against you. You are warned that if you fail to do so the case may proceed without you and a judgment may be entered against you by the court without further notice for any money claimed in the complaint or for any other claim or relief requested by the plaintiff. You may lose money or property or other rights important to you.

YOU SHOULD TAKE THIS PAPER TO YOUR LAWYER AT ONCE. IF YOU DO NOT HAVE A LAWYER, GO TO OR TELEPHONE THE OFFICE

SET FORTH BELOW. THIS OFFICE CAN PROVIDE YOU WITH INFORMATION ABOUT HIRING A LAWYER.

IF YOU CANNOT AFFORD TO HIRE A LAWYER, THIS OFFICE MAY BE ABLE TO PROVIDE YOU WITH INFORMATION ABOUT AGENCIES THAT MAY OFFER LEGAL SERVICES TO ELIGIBLE PERSONS AT A REDUCED FEE OR NO FEE.

This is not meant to be a complete recitation of the possible issues that arise in various jurisdictions, but is a "heads up" to make sure you know what must be included in your filing package.

4. Inconsistent Causes of Action

Are you subject to sanctions for inconsistent causes of action? F.R.C.P. 8(d) specifically allows inconsistent pleadings:

(2) Alternative Statements of a Claim or Defense. A party may set out two or more statements of a claim or defense alternatively or hypothetically, either in a single count or defense or in separate ones. If a party makes alternative statements, the pleading is sufficient if any one of them is sufficient.

(3) Inconsistent Claims or Defenses. A party may state as many separate claims or defenses as it has, regardless of consistency.

Most jurisdictions have the same rule. But remember that you are still subject to the provisions of the courts' rules on sanctions; you can't plead that the traffic light was red for the plaintiff and that it was green for the plaintiff unless you don't know which it was. If the same set of facts that you do know can be interpreted to allow for inconsistent relief, and you claim the inconsistent relief, you won't be sanctioned. In other words, be honest.

Be sure that you have included in your complaint all the causes of action that arise out of the set of facts you have; if you don't, those claims can be forever extinguished. In New Jersey, this rule is called the Entire Controversy Doctrine. See Rule 4:30A: "Non-joinder of claims required to be joined by the entire controversy doctrine shall result in the preclusion of the omitted claims to the extent required by the entire controversy doctrine. . ."

The federal rules do not specifically address compulsory claims in a complaint: "The entire controversy doctrine is more preclusive than *res judicata*." Lubrizol Corp. v. Exxon Corp., 929 F.2d 960, 965 (3d Cir. 1991). However, as discussed below, F.R.C.P. 13 requires certain counterclaims to be brought or lost.

5. Service

Be sure to follow the rules on serving the complaint. Each jurisdiction is different. You want to be sure that you have achieved proper and timely service of the complaint.

6. Amendments

Despite all your best efforts to gather the facts, and to determine what causes of action your client has, what if you discover after filing the complaint some new fact or claim that should be in the complaint? Most jurisdictions have a fail-safe mechanism for amending the complaint, usually as long as the defendant hasn't answered or moved to dismiss ("filed a responsive pleading"). The plaintiff may also amend as a matter of course (in contrast to with court permission) in response to a defense motion to dismiss or an answer that raises issues that you can remedy by amending the complaint. See, for example, F.R.C.P. 15:

> (1) A party may amend its pleading once as a matter of course within:
>
> (A) 21 days after serving it, or
>
> (B) if the pleading is one to which a responsive pleading is required, 21 days after service of a responsive pleading or 21 days after service of a motion under Rule 12(b), (e), or (f), whichever is earlier.

At any point in the litigation, if events have occurred since you filed the complaint or if new facts have come to light, through discovery or in some other fashion, you may ask the court for permission to amend. In some jurisdictions, such as federal court, you may amend by agreement with your adversary. See F.R.C.P. 15(2): "In all other cases, a party may amend its pleading only with the opposing party's written consent or the court's leave. The court should freely give leave when justice so requires." The best practice is to move for permission to amend, attaching the proposed amended pleading.

7. The Key

Remember that the key to drafting a complaint is to fit in the essentials without creating a dry, uninteresting document.

Dry versus Wet Pleadings, Part 2

If you want the judge or her clerk to read the complaint with anything like interest, you should tell a story. Some lawyers, and I include myself in this category, begin complaints with a section called something like "The Background." The numbered paragraphs of this section set out the client's view of the facts as if it were a novel. If all goes well and discovery bears out the client's view, this story will become the basis of your opening statement to the jury and your closing argument.

The story here does not use legalese. It sounds like this:

1. In 1985, Pittsburgh began to become a mecca for financial services. New employees flocked to the city, looking for work and a place to live. Plaintiff Harry Winslow decided to buy farmland property on the outskirts of Pittsburgh to build houses for these new Pittsburghers. He looked for land that was green and had never been used for industry, so he wouldn't have to worry about cleaning up any pollution when he was building houses.

Part Two

DRAFTING A RESPONSE

Before You Begin

Let's say that your client is now on the receiving end of a well-written, compelling complaint. What do you do?

A. Deadlines

First of all, be sure you know when the response to the complaint is due. The time varies for response by jurisdiction. You also must make sure that your client didn't sit on the complaint for most of the time and you now have one day to file a response. Believe me, most clients are clueless about the fact that there is a due date. Some clients have such labyrinthine office procedures that a complaint won't get to a decision-maker to send to a lawyer until past the due date.

If you are up against a response deadline, you may have some options. In some jurisdictions, you have the right to an automatic extension, and can extend the time merely by filing a request for an extension. In others, you may need to obtain your opponent's agreement to an extension. Each jurisdiction has its own requirements with respect to the underpinnings for an extension, such as "good cause," whatever that is. (Despite attempts to define "good cause," most courts simply abide by the gut test to determine if there is a good excuse for failure to respond.) Failing all else, you can petition the court for the right to file a response. In some jurisdictions, the best practice is to attach your response to the request for an extension, in order to demonstrate to the court that you are not purposely delaying.

When a client comes to you with a complaint that has been properly served for which the response time has run,

Do You Answer The Complaint? Or Do You Respond?

There are generally three ways to respond to a complaint:

1. Answer
2. Move to dismiss some or all of the complaint
3. Move for a more definite statement

If you are in state court, you may also be able to move to remove the case to federal court; if you are in federal court, you may be able to move to remand to state court. Which of these avenues you choose will have ramifications throughout the remainder of the case, and the choice is one of the most important strategic decisions you can make as a defendant.

Each of these choices is a "response" to the complaint, and you may hear them referred to, or read that they are identified in your rules as, "responsive pleadings."

the first thing you should do vis-à-vis the client is to prepare a retention letter saying the client acknowledges that you did not receive the complaint in time to respond, and that you will not be liable if the time for response is not extended.

B. Extensions

As I mentioned, in some jurisdictions a defendant is entitled to one automatic extension to file a response. What if you need a plaintiff's agreement for an extension?

There is a golden rule in the practice of law which is pretty much the same as the version of the golden rule in life: do unto others as you would have them do unto you. You can ask your opponent for an extension, and if your opponent refuses, you can retaliate by refusing your opponent's request for something later during the case (like an extra few weeks to answer interrogatories). Because almost everyone abides by the golden rule, you will most likely not have a problem asking for and receiving an extension. If you do receive an extension, put it in writing. It will most likely be called a "Stipulation to Extend Time."

Unfortunately, there are jerks in the legal profession who play hardball. In that case, where plaintiff's counsel refuses to grant an extension, you will have to appeal to the court. Again, in most cases, the court will grant an extension, unless pure evil or gross negligence caused the defendant to fail to answer the complaint. Nevertheless, don't count on your opponent's or the court's good will. There is still no guarantee that you will be allowed to answer a complaint beyond the time allotted by rule.

There is one more thing to be wary of. One of my law partners, an extremely able and experienced lawyer, fell into this trap. He asked his opponent in a case for an extension of time to answer the complaint. His opponent sent him a written stipulation "extending the time to answer the complaint." My partner signed and filed the stipulation. My partner then filed a motion to dismiss, and the lawyer for the plaintiff objected on the ground that the extension was only for an answer, not for a motion. The plaintiff moved to have the motion stricken, and he was successful. Then my partner was forced to answer the complaint, even though he believed the client could have succeeded on a motion to dismiss, which the court never got to hear. The lesson is that there is a difference between an answer and a response, and you want the more encompassing noun "response" in your stipulation to extend time: "The parties stip-

Time Is of The Essence

Don't forget that every litigation has time limits for everything. As a defendant, the first one you'll face for your client is responding to the complaint. Blowing a time limit can lead to a significant malpractice verdict against YOU. Docket every due date in your electronic calendar and, if you're lucky enough to have one, a docketing program that will send you emails reminding you of your due dates. Don't rely on memory.

And don't rely on your client. Some clients think due dates are mere suggestions, not mandates.

ulate that defendant has an additional 20 days in which to file a response to the complaint."

Some clients believe that court deadlines and due dates are not mandatory, but merely suggestions. You must train these clients that due dates are to be taken seriously, or they may face having a judgment entered against them.

You may find that because your client hasn't come to you in time to respond to the complaint, the plaintiff has already entered judgment for failure to respond. In some jurisdictions, a plaintiff must go through a two-step process before entering judgment for failure to respond—first, taking a default against the defendant, with notice, and then after notice and no action from the defendant, a default judgment. Depending on what stage this debacle has reached, you may have to petition the court to open the default or the judgment to allow the defendant to defend himself.

The rules vary so much from one jurisdiction to another that I can only point you once again to the rules of the court you're in to determine how to deal with defaults.

C. The Poorly-Written Complaint

Occasionally, you or your client will receive a complaint that is so poorly written, you have no idea what the plaintiff wants. This creates a dilemma as to how to respond. Do you move to dismiss, as is discussed below? Do you move for a more definite statement, also discussed below? Or do you try to figure out what's going on, and answer the complaint?

Each of these paths has its benefits. I believe, however, that strategically it makes more sense to contact the lawyer for the plaintiff, or the plaintiff if the plaintiff is pro se, to determine the underlying basis of the complaint. Your client may even know who the plaintiff is and what the plaintiff's claims are, no matter how poorly expressed. Sure, you can move to dismiss, or move for a more definite statement, ridiculing the poor draftsmanship in your motions, but what will the likely outcome be? Most often, a judge will grant the plaintiff leave to amend. So all you have done is delay the day of reckoning for your client, and add legal fees that may not be necessary (even if you personally enjoy the fruits).

On the other hand, if you discuss this issue with the pro se plaintiff or plaintiff's lawyer, you may be able to agree on an amended complaint that fairly states the claim or claims. This should not be seen as "caving in" or "helping the plaintiff." It is you and your client who will be best served by having a complaint to respond to.

Of course, you may have an intransigent plaintiff who won't cooperate, or who can't cooperate because of mental illness or illiteracy. In that case, you will have to seek the court's help by filing a motion to dismiss. The Court in Moser v. State of Oklahoma, had no hesitation dismissing an incomprehensible complaint, and the Tenth Circuit Court of Appeals affirmed, based on the plaintiff's gobbledygook, which it quoted verbatim:

> The petition Habeas Corpus, Writ, was initially, placed to produce a hearing, to determine legal cause, for the disapperance of the plaintiff's

antique coins, which could only be answered by, personnal attendance, to the court. Also the indefferece, to the Law, reguarding, protection, equally, according, to the Constitution of the United States, given those rights. Rights, when taken away, can be compensated, for by civil action

Pursuant to, Title 42, U.S.C. 1983, Civil Rights, the plaintiff, made a claim by petition, stating pertinent facts, concerning his rights being violated. Defendant's rebuttel (Brief in Chief), in his own words, (In short, assuming arguendo, a claim pursuant to 1983, could be discerned from the complaint.), a dismissal, should not be gained by, this statement, accordingly.

This action, in the Supreme Court, 10th Circuit, is, the failure of, this State's, leaders, to promote, truth, honesty, integrity, in personnel chosen, to maintain the highest system, of our state, the Judicary. Corruption has become, the mainstem, of thier existance. If you don't pay, you don't win your case. accusations, of bribery and indecency, has been reported, on our local television news station.

The experience, in these documents, are a testimony to that leadership. By the grace of God, I'am aloud to place this, prima face evidence, in your hands. The pressure has escalated, to the point, I can no longer achieve my goals.

> Individuals, named in this package, are watching, as I work and they copy all materials, I prepare for court. This knowledge of my writtings, flow out, to everone, that has a position, to cancel or dismiss, all efforts, to gain releif.
>
> Oppression of one's rights, are hard to over-come, as these six years, have passed.

Quoted in Slip Opinion, No. 04-6127.

I have received barely comprehensible pleadings very similar to Mr. Moser's, and when I do, it makes my heart sink, because I know that getting rid of the complaint is likely to be a drawn out process for the client. Let your client know, should you receive one of these, that patience is a virtue. She will have to wait through the unfolding of the drama, as you move to dismiss, the court grants plaintiff time to file an amended complaint, the amended complaint is just as bad, you move to dismiss. . . . You get the idea. Even in our post-Twombly era, where plausibility is purportedly required in a complaint, a court will usually allow a disjointed pleader a do-over, sometimes even more than one.

Although it is one of the burdens that comes with our system of justice, I wouldn't have it any other way; it means that everyone, even the mentally ill, has access to our courts.

D. Fact Investigation

Your client tells you he is shocked, shocked by his receipt of the complaint. It makes no sense, the plaintiff has no claim against him. What do you do?

Just like when you were preparing to draft a complaint, you must do some preparatory work. And this includes doing a factual investigation beyond what your client tells you. If the complaint involves a contract, you must read the contract and its surrounding documents. If the complaint involves an automobile accident, look for police reports and photographs. You have a duty not to lie in your answer to the complaint.

But wait, I hear you say. How can I possibly be sure I have the facts right when the time to answer a complaint is usually short?

Luckily, there is some wiggle room available in the art of answering a complaint. This wiggle room is often phrased something like this (again, depending on your local practice or court rules): "Defendant, after reasonable investigation, is without knowledge or information sufficient to form a belief as to the truth of the averment." See, for example, Pa. R. Civ. Pro. 1029(c). This is different from an outright denial, although it has the effect of denying the allegation. And using this terminology means that later, after discovery has taken place, if you find that the allegation is true, you haven't lied.

However, a defendant cannot use lack of knowledge or information to skate away from an answer when the defendant actually knows whether the allegation is true or false. For example, where a complaint alleges that defendant is married to the plaintiff, it is bad faith of the worst sort to say defendant doesn't know if it's true.

In those jurisdictions, such as the federal system, where both plaintiffs and defendants must make rather sub-

Sometimes Clients Lie

Despite your best efforts as an officer of the court to tell the truth, sometimes you will be up against an unfortunate fact: some clients lie. There is nothing worse than facing a plaintiff who knows your client is lying when you believe him to be telling the truth.

An unfortunate example from my youth: I was representing a distributor of women's coats. His supplier had sent him 200 raincoats. My client refused to pay for them, saying they were defective and that he'd had to sell them at a steep discount to get rid of them. The supposed defect was that the pockets were put in backwards. That's what I said in my answer to the complaint and in the new matter asserting affirmative defenses (about which, more below under "Defenses v. Denials"). I discovered, upon reading the plaintiff's answer to my new matter, that the pockets were supposed to be backwards to keep rainwater from entering them. When I asked my client about this, he admitted that he knew the pockets were in the right position.

stantial disclosures at the pleading stage, before discovery occurs, you will often have enough information to answer the complaint.

E. The Law

Your prep work, before you decide whether to answer or to move to dismiss, includes an analysis of the law involved in the plaintiff's claims. You must take into account what are, essentially, the reciprocals of those considerations necessary to prepare a complaint. For example, if the plaintiff has brought a federal claim in state court, the court has no jurisdiction over the suit. As I discussed earlier, certain claims can only be decided in federal district court: "The district courts shall have original jurisdiction of all civil actions arising under the Constitution, laws or treaties of the United States." Title 28 U.S.C. Section 1331.

Has the plaintiff properly pleaded a claim against the defendant? Assuming that the complaint is comprehensible, did the plaintiff properly allege each element of each cause of action asserted against the defendant?

Has the statute of limitations run? It is your duty as the legal professional to ensure that your client is protected from stale claims. It may be that certain claims are stale and others are not, but you should assert the running of the statute for those causes that are no longer viable. These kinds of analyses will help you determine if you should answer the complaint or move to dismiss.

Has the plaintiff failed to include in the lawsuit all necessary parties? The necessary party concept is found in all jurisdictions, state and federal, and if the plaintiff has not sued a required, necessary party, the case often will be dismissed. For example, in Alabama, the absence of an indispensable party is a jurisdictional defect that renders the proceeding void. See Gilbert v. Nicholson, 845 So. 2d 785, 790 (Ala. 2002). In the federal courts, Rules 19 and 20 define which parties must be joined. The court's goal under this rubric is to ensure that complete relief can be accorded to all interested parties and that no one who is not a party will be subjected to multiple suits on the same subject matter.

F. Use It Or Lose It

Apart from the defense of lack of subject matter jurisdiction, you must raise all of your defenses in a responsive pleading or they will be deemed to be waived. See F.R.C.P. 12(g) and (h).

What An Answer Looks Like

[Same caption as the complaint]

Answer
[See Sample Complaint, page 8, to which this is an answer]

1. Admitted.
2. Admitted.
3. It is denied that defendant breached a contract with plaintiff. To the extent this allegation is a conclusion of law, no response is required, and it is deemed to be denied.

Count One

xx. Defendant repeats here its answers to paragraphs 1-xix, as if fully set forth, and incorporates them by reference.

xxi. Etc.

WHEREFORE defendant demands judgment in its favor and against plaintiff on count one of the complaint, and an award of attorneys' fees and costs, together with whatever relief the court deems just.

Deciding on Your Strategy

Chapter Four

Do you answer the complaint or do you move to dismiss it? This is one of the most important and complex decisions you will make at the beginning of your involvement in this case. The basis of your decision depends on the availability of certain legal defenses as well as on strategic considerations.

I use the phrase "legal defenses" because if your client's defense is fact-based (e.g., "the defendant already paid the debt the plaintiff is seeking to collect"), it is no longer a preliminary matter that can be determined by a motion to dismiss. A fact defense usually has to await the unfolding of discovery, at which point the defendant can move for summary judgment based on the record.

Again, the local rules vary with respect to some defenses and whether they must be raised in an answer or in a motion to dismiss (or, in a state like Pennsylvania, via preliminary objections or petition, depending on the issue). Be sure you know your rules of procedure.

An important thing to remember is: use it or lose it! You must raise all defenses in a responsive pleading or risk waiving them. See, for example, F.R.C.P. 12; N.J.R. Civ. Pro. 4:6-2. In federal court, there are so-called "compulsory cross-claims," see F.R.C.P. 13, and in state courts possibly some other nomenclature is used. As I mentioned above, New Jersey has the Entire Controversy Doctrine, which applies to all claims, cross-claims and counterclaims; you must raise all defenses or claims at once, or waive them. See, for example, N.J.R. Civ. Pro. 4:7-5. As the commentary to that rule makes clear,

> The mandatory joinder requirements imposed by the entire controversy doctrine are expressly incorporated into this rule, requiring the pleading or consequent waiver of all cross-claims and counterclaims asserting causes of action constituting a component part of the transaction or series of transactions pleaded in the complaint.

Comment 2.

If you file a motion to dismiss, it will alter the time frames for answering the complaint. Filing the motion "tolls" the time set out in the rules; the motion serves as an alternative to the answer. Once the court rules on your motion, you will have to answer any remaining claims within a new time period set by the rules. In federal court, the defendant must answer any remaining claims within 14 days of the court's disposition of the motion to dismiss. See F.R.C.P. 12(a)(4).

A. Lack of Subject Matter Jurisdiction

Although your local rules will guide you about the form your defenses should take (i.e., motion to dismiss, affirmative defenses, preliminary objections), there is one ironclad rule: if there is no subject matter jurisdiction, the action must be dismissed. This is true everywhere, as it rises to the level of a constitutional mandate. You should assert this at the outset of the litigation in a motion to dismiss. Since subject matter jurisdiction cannot be waived, even if the defendant doesn't assert it, a lawsuit can be thrown out as late as after trial and appeal if the court determines it had no right to hear the case in the first place. "If the court determines at any time that it lacks subject-matter jurisdiction, the court must dismiss the action." F.R.C.P. 12(h)(3). Notice that mandatory language again!

What Are Your Defenses?

Generally, the following defenses are available in every jurisdiction:

1. Lack of subject matter jurisdiction
2. Lack of personal jurisdiction
3. Improper venue
4. Failure to state a claim (legal insufficiency of the pleading)
5. Improper service or failure of service
6. Insufficient specificity of the pleading
7. Lack of capacity to sue
8. Failure to join a necessary party

If the court has no jurisdiction, you should not waste your time answering the complaint. This is a clear case for you to file a motion to dismiss. If you don't, and you should have, your client will be justifiably pissed at remaining in the case and racking up fees. In fact, failure to move to dismiss on this ground may subject you to a malpractice suit.

B. Lack of Personal Jurisdiction

If it seems unfair to you that your client has to defend a lawsuit in the jurisdiction chosen by the plaintiff—if, for example, the defendant resides and works in California, but has been sued in Delaware—you may have the legal defense of lack of jurisdiction over the person. This is also known as "in personam jurisdiction." Whether or not the plaintiff has the right to sue the defendant where he did is both a legal and a factual issue.

The issue of your client's amenability to suit in the court chosen by the plaintiff is intertwined with the issue of sufficiency of service of process, although your client could be amenable to suit and the plaintiff's service of process can still be defective. A state's long-arm statute or local service rules will determine if the plaintiff has the right to stretch the long arm of the law over your client. See, for example, N.J.R. Civ. Pro. 4:4-4 and commentary.

Long-arm statutes vest the state courts with the ability to assert jurisdiction over a defendant to the outer limits of due process. Each jurisdiction has developed its own body of law as to what constitutes the "fundamental fairness" of these outer limits. Often, but not always, there must be minimum contacts with the locale such that forcing the defendant into court does not offend "traditional notions of fair play and substantial justice." International Shoe Co. v. Washington, 326 U.S. 310 (1945). In the Internet age, a defendant's forum-related contacts can be as minimal as selling an item to a plaintiff in cyberspace.

Also, unlike subject matter jurisdiction, personal jurisdiction can be created by agreement of the parties, and the parties to a contract can set forth the court in which their disputes are to be heard and agree to submit to the jurisdiction of that particular court.

Assuming that your client did not agree to the personal jurisdiction of the court he's been sued in, and that there are no other grounds for his presence in that court, should you move to dismiss or should you answer the complaint?

The central problem is this: do you subject your client to the personal jurisdiction of the court by entering an appearance on his behalf, by answering a complaint, by filing a motion to dismiss? The answer in all jurisdictions used to be that your client was between a rock and a hard place. If his position was that he was not subject to the personal jurisdiction of the court, then he should remain silent and allow a default to be taken. However, if he was wrong—that is, a court later determined that he was subject to its jurisdiction—he was out of luck, because he could only contest the court's jurisdiction over him, and could not litigate the underlying merits of the suit. In some jurisdictions, a defendant could protect himself by filing a so-called "special appearance" solely for the purpose of contesting jurisdiction.

Rule 12 of the Federal Rules changed this Catch-22 for the federal courts. It sets out personal jurisdiction as one of seven defenses that can be joined together in either a motion or an answer, and provides that "No defense or objection is waived by joining it with one or more other defenses or objections in a responsive pleading or in a motion." F.R.C.P. 12(b).

Most state courts have since followed suit.

> "The special appearance is a device formerly used under the civil rules to contest the existence of personal jurisdiction. A defendant making a special appearance had to take care to avoid any inconsistent action that might serve to waive the jurisdictional objection and convert the special appearance into a general appearance. Today, however, the rules of civil procedure permit a defendant to contest the existence of personal jurisdiction and to contest the merits of the action as well. Therefore, the special appearance has been largely abandoned in civil practice."

MoKan Dial, Inc. v. Sprint Missouri, Inc. et al., TC-2002-182 (PSC MO 2002).

Some jurisdictions, however, still have the special appearance rule, and you must determine if yours is one of them.

C. Failure of Service

As I mentioned above, the issue of personal jurisdiction is intertwined with the issue of proper service. Because of some activity of the defendant in the forum, she may be amenable to suit, but if she is not properly served, she is not a part of the lawsuit. By the same token, a defendant may be properly served, for example by personal service in the forum, and yet not be subject to the jurisdiction of the court because of the absence of forum-related activities. In other words, long-arm jurisdiction can fail either because the defendant has no forum-related activities that subject her to suit or because the plaintiff never properly served her. You must assert the defense of failure of service in your initial responsive pleading or it will be waived.

This seems very dry, doesn't it? But in the real world, the consequences of improper service can be quite dramatic. I represented a Spanish company with headquarters in Madrid that was informed of a $13 million default judgment that had been taken against it because the company failed to appear in court. The president of the company didn't deny that he knew his company had been sued in federal court in the United States, but he said he hadn't been properly served with process. His decision to ignore attempts to serve him in Spain, which he had done on the advice of his company's general counsel, resulted in a "bet the company" situation, since the company did business in the United States. The company's president was concerned that the plaintiff would ultimately serve process on a company representative when he entered the country to attend the Academy Awards, subjecting the company to enforcement proceedings on the $13 million judgment.

The short version of the story is that the district court judge denied my motion to open the default, and I ultimately had to take the matter to the Third Circuit Court of Appeals, where I prevailed on the ground of failure of service. The long version involves, among other things, the Hague Convention, the use of notaries in Spain, and Pennsylvania's long-arm jurisdiction and its rules on service of process. (See the accompanying box, "Failure of Service of Process—the longer version.") And, oh yes, then Judge, now Justice, Samuel Alito of the United States Supreme Court was on the panel that was on my side. The company paid me much less in attorneys' fees than the $13 million they would have been required to pay the plaintiff.

D. Failure to State A Claim

If your legal research convinces you that the plaintiff has not pleaded all the elements of a cause of action, or has not pleaded them properly, you should assert the defense of failure to state a claim upon which relief may be granted. You may assert this in your answer or you may choose to file a motion to dismiss. Under the federal rules, and in most state courts as well, if you decide to assert the defense by motion, you must make it before you file an answer. For example, see Rule 12 (b), F.R.C.P.: "A motion asserting any of [the defenses 12(b) (1) through (7)] must be made before pleading if a responsive pleading is allowed." Again, as we all remember from law school, that word "must" is mandatory.

In many cases, a judge will allow a plaintiff to replead a defective complaint. However, as the Twombly and Iqbal line of cases has shown us, some courts have become draconian about pleading requirements, and may not allow a plaintiff to amend a complaint. If you have that kind of

Failure of Service of Process—The Longer Version

I was contacted by a Spanish corporation that licensed Spanish movies to distributors in the United States. The company had been sued in federal court in the Eastern District of Pennsylvania for $13 million by a film distributor. The company president believed he had not been properly served and failed to respond to the lawsuit. The district court entered a $13 million default judgment after repeated failure of the defendant to appear. I accepted the matter and delved into the facts about service.

Plaintiff had followed the Hague convention then in effect, had translated the complaint papers into Spanish and had a "notario," a cross between a notary and a lawyer, take the complaint to the company's headquarters in Madrid. However, it was August, and no one was at headquarters; everyone was on vacation. The notario left the papers with the building's receptionist. The receptionist was not an employee of my client, was not authorized to accept service, and simply tended the building for all the tenants.

In federal court, long-arm jurisdiction is a matter of the forum state's law. This was not good service under Pennsylvania law, which required that service of process had to be accomplished by handing it to the person in charge of the office, even if that person was a secretary. And it was not good service under Spanish law or under the Hague convention. My defense involved a great deal of unusual research, which was fun, by the way. And although it didn't convince the district court judge, who held that service was proper, it did convince the Court of Appeals, which vacated the default judgment.

judge, or if the caselaw in your jurisdiction leads you to believe that you have a good chance at succeeding on a motion to dismiss for failure to state a claim, it is surely in your client's best interest to file such a motion, and not to simply append the defense to an answer. The latter course involves more time and legal fees, which may make your client unhappy.

E. Defenses versus Denials

Your defendant may have fact defenses, legal defenses, denials, new matter, separate defenses—every jurisdiction has its own nomenclature for defenses and its own rules about how defenses are to be raised. If your defense is not of the kind that is case-dispositive at the very outset (e.g., lack of subject matter jurisdiction), you are not going to be filing a motion to dismiss. But how do you raise your defenses? Do you just deny the allegations of the complaint in your answer? Do you bring new facts into the mix in your answer? And if so, where do you put these new facts? And what do you call the section of the answer where you raise the new facts? The answer to these questions lie, of course, in the rules of the jurisdiction you're in.

For example, in Pennsylvania some defenses are called "new matter" and must be so labeled:

> Rule 1030. New Matter.
>
> (a) Except as provided by subdivision (b), all affirmative defenses including but not limited to the defenses of accord and satisfaction,

> arbitration and award, consent, discharge in bankruptcy, duress, estoppel, failure of consideration, fair comment, fraud, illegality, immunity from suit, impossibility of performance, justification, laches, license, payment, privilege, release, res judicata, statute of frauds, statute of limitations, truth and waiver shall be pleaded in a responsive pleading under the heading "New Matter." A party may set forth as new matter any other material facts which are not merely denials of the averments of the preceding pleading.
>
> (b) The affirmative defenses of assumption of the risk, comparative negligence and contributory negligence need not be pleaded.

There is no way a lawyer could know, without looking at the Pennsylvania rules of civil procedure, that the named defenses in Rule 1030 are to be labeled "new matter." Similarly, if you are in New Jersey (just across the river, I might add, from Pennsylvania), you wouldn't know which defenses to label "affirmative defenses" unless you look at N.J.R. Civ. Pro. 4:5-4:

> A responsive pleading shall set forth specifically and separately a statement of facts constituting an avoidance or affirmative defense such as accord and satisfaction, arbitration and award, contributory negligence, discharge in bankruptcy, duress, estoppel, failure of consideration, fraud,

> illegality, injury by fellow servant, laches, license, payment, release, res judicata, statute of frauds, statute of limitations, and waiver. If a party has mistakenly designated a defense as a counterclaim or a counterclaim as a defense, the court, on terms if the interest of justice requires, shall treat the pleading as if there had been a proper designation.

Let me boil down my point to what I repeatedly mention in this book: read the rules for the jurisdiction you're in.

F. Venue, Removal, Remand

You will want to determine if your defendant client has a choice of forum, and if so, where. If you are in state court but believe your client's case has a better chance of success in federal court, the federal removal statute, 28 U.S.C. 1446, allows removal to federal from state court as long as all the plaintiffs have diverse citizenship from all the defendants. For example, as long as the plaintiff lives in Pennsylvania and the defendant is incorporated in Delaware, there is complete diversity.

By contrast, if your client has been sued in federal court and you believe he would be better served in state court, you may be able to move to remand the case to state court under 28 U.S.C. Section 1447. One of the grounds for such remand is that there is no diversity of citizenship, a case that can occur when a non-diverse party has been joined by plaintiff or brought in as a third party by a defendant. I will discuss more about third party practice below.

Drafting The Answer

Before I knew about consulting the civil procedural rules, life was easy. I received a complaint and, on behalf of my client, I'd just deny everything:

"Count 1 (trespass): paragraphs 1-8 are denied."

Luckily for me and for the client, because I was only a first-year associate at the time, a supervising lawyer took one look at the answer and pointed me back to the rules. He also, thankfully, gave me an answer that he had just completed in another matter so I could get with the program.

A. Answering The Numbered Paragraphs

Every jurisdiction has its own customs in addition to its own rules. As a result, the rules will tell you what you must do to answer the allegations of a complaint, but not how that looks on the page. Thus, Pennsylvania Rule 1029, in relevant part states:

> (a) A responsive pleading shall admit or deny each averment of fact in the preceding

pleading or any part thereof to which it is responsive. A party denying only a part of an averment shall specify so much of it as is admitted and shall deny the remainder. Admissions and denials in a responsive pleading shall refer specifically to the paragraph in which the averment admitted or denied is set forth.

(b) Averments in a pleading to which a responsive pleading is required are admitted when not denied specifically or by necessary implication. A general denial or a demand for proof, except as provided by subdivision (c) and (e) of this rule, shall have the effect of an admission.

(c) A statement by a party that after reasonable investigation the party is without knowledge or information sufficient to form a belief as the truth of an averment shall have the effect of a denial.

Official Note

Reliance on subdivision (c) does not excuse a failure to admit or deny a factual allegation when it is clear that the pleader must know whether a particular allegation is true or false. See Cercone v. Cercone, 254 Pa. Super. 381, 386 A.2d 1 (1978).

(d) Averments in a pleading to which no responsive pleading is required shall be deemed to be denied.

Looking at this rule now, I realize that if I didn't already know now what it means, I wouldn't know what it means. The explanation is too dense. The example of an answer that I received from the supervising attorney showed me what all of that wordage meant.

So, a simple statement of fact in a complaint, if not true, can be denied. But it can't be denied the way I tried to do it all those many years ago. Instead, a fair denial is:

> "6. Defendant denies the allegations of paragraph 6 of the complaint, as she does not live at 50 Rockefeller Center, New York, NY."

However, if defendant lives at Rockefeller Center, just not at number 50, you must explain your denial.

> "6. Defendant denies the allegation of paragraph 6 of the complaint, to the extent it alleges she lives at 50 Rockefeller Center. Defendant's address is in fact 51 Rockefeller Center."

If the statement in the complaint doesn't require a responsive pleading, according to the Pennsylvania rule, it is "deemed" to be denied. What is this all about?

Statements of law do not require responsive pleading. If the complaint states the law incorrectly, the judge will "fix" it. The defendant isn't required to point out legal principles. (Of course, in some situations, the defendant will want to argue that the complaint is legally deficient, in which case, as I discuss above, you will file a motion to dismiss on the defendant's behalf.)

This does not mean that you can safely ignore a legal allegation, and just skip it in your answer. Here is where custom comes in. Every Pennsylvania lawyer worth his or her salt knows that the proper way to address an allegation of law is as follows:

> "7. The allegations of paragraph 7 of the complaint are conclusions of law to which no response is required, and they are deemed to be denied."

Lawyers like us can never be silent on a topic when twenty-five words are available.

What is an allegation of law? Suppose the plaintiff alleges that your defendant client negligently drove his car and rear-ended the plaintiff. In order to demonstrate negligence in the complaint, the plaintiff will have to allege many facts, such as: "Defendant failed to stop in time because he was texting on his iPhone." This is clearly a factual allegation. It will have to be proved or disproved during the course of the litigation. By contrast, after a recitation of facts in the complaint, when the plaintiff alleges "Defendant was negligent in driving his car," the allegation is a legal conclusion. Why? Because negligence is a legal concept. And the finder of fact will determine if the plaintiff has made out the facts that support that allegation. The judge will decide if the plaintiff has met his burden to prove the legal concept of negligence.

What if you're not sure if an allegation is legal or factual? Or what if the allegation is both? For example, a plaintiff may write in her complaint: "Defendant negligently drove his car in an unsafe manner because he was texting while he drove." In such a case, you must respond to the allegation both as to facts and as to law. Thus:

> "7. To the extent this paragraph is a conclusion of law, no response is required, and it is deemed to be denied. To the extent this paragraph alleges that defendant was texting while driving, it is denied."

On behalf of your client, you must answer every numbered paragraph of the complaint, including those retrospective paragraphs at the beginning of each count. Thus, if the complaint says:

> "10. Paragraphs 1-9 are realleged here as if fully set forth."

Your answer will read:

> "10. Paragraphs 1-9 of this answer are realleged here as if fully set forth."

Even the unnumbered "Wherefore" or ad damnum clause must be answered. Where Plaintiff says:

> "Wherefore, plaintiff demands judgment on Count I against defendant."

Your answer will read:

> "Wherefore, defendant demands judgment on Count I in his favor and against plaintiff."

B. Answering The "Speaking Complaint"

What if the complaint tells a story? (In other words, what if your opponent takes my advice and makes the complaint interesting?) How do you handle more than plain vanilla allegations?

You have two choices: answer each sentence of a speaking complaint separately as I have described above, or answer each paragraph with a story of your own. Sometimes, you must do both. Here's what I mean.

Let's take the paragraph from the speaking complaint above, about Harry Winslow.

> "1. In 1985, Pittsburgh began to become a mecca for financial services. New employees flocked to the city, looking for work and a place to live. Plaintiff Harry Winslow decided to buy farmland property on the outskirts of Pittsburgh to build houses for these new Pittsburghers. He looked for land that was green and had never been used for industry, so he wouldn't have to worry about cleaning up any pollution when he was building houses."

You can answer this in the traditional manner:

> "1. After reasonable investigation, defendant is without sufficient information to form a belief as to the truth of these allegations, and if relevant, strict proof is demanded."

Or you can counter with a story of your own, while following the rules of pleading for answers:

"1. Denied as stated. To the contrary, by 1985, Pittsburgh's economy was already beginning to slow down, and many fewer new employees were entering the workforce. As to plaintiff's motives and beliefs, defendant is without information and cannot form a belief as to the truth of these allegations, and if relevant, strict proof is demanded."

Your answer to the complaint will not give you a full opportunity to tell your client's story. For that, you will need to draft counterclaims, if you have them, or affirmative defenses, about both of which more below.

C. Affirmative Defenses

As I mentioned above, your local rules will tell you which defenses are to be labeled "new matter" or "affirmative defenses." Assuming your jurisdiction calls all defenses "affirmative defenses," your answer to the complaint will include a section titled, not surprisingly, "Affirmative Defenses." Each locale has its own peculiarities about numbering, but in general the numbering for defenses begins again at "1."

So your defenses section will look like this:

Affirmative Defenses

1. Defendant Church is not liable for the contract damages claimed by plaintiff because defendant already paid the sum claimed.
2. The statute of limitations has run on the debt claimed by plaintiff.

3. The debt is owed to plaintiff by a third party over whom defendant has no control.

You will list every conceivable defense in this section, even if you have alluded to it previously in the numbered paragraphs of your answer, and even if you will be repeating them in your counterclaim. If you don't plead your affirmative defenses, you waive them. See, e.g., F.R.C.P. 12(g) and (h).

For those of us lucky enough to have heard the late, great Irving Younger lecture, we remember the affirmative defenses he used as an example, to show that the defenses can be inconsistent as long as they are all possibly true, to wit:

> Take the simplest case you can imagine. A farmer has a patch of cabbages. His neighbor has a goat. The goat breaks loose, gets in the cabbage patch and eats all the cabbages. The farmer brings a lawsuit against his neighbor. He says, 'I had a patch of cabbages worth $100. Your goat ate my cabbages. Give me my $100."

And the defendant says:

> "You had no cabbages. If you had any cabbages, they were not eaten. If your cabbages were eaten, it was not by a goat. If your cabbages were eaten by a goat, it wasn't my goat. And if it was my goat, he was insane!"

As told by the late Bob Hanley in closing argument in MCI v. AT&T.

As Ralph Waldo Emerson wrote, "A foolish consistency is the hobgoblin of little minds. . ."

Of course, if your case gets to trial, you will want to winnow your affirmative defenses down to one, or maybe two, lest the judge or jury thinks your client is unsure of himself and trying too hard to get out from under the claims. (I once quoted this Emersonian wisdom to a judge during a hearing. The judge seemed not to understand what I was trying to say, and thought I was calling him a hobgoblin, or implying that he had a little mind. That incident taught me to speak plainly and save quotations for some other forum.)

Some local rules specifically provide that if you have misdesignated a defense as a counterclaim, the judge can save your bacon. See, for example, N.J.R. Civ. Pro. 4:5-4. Not every jurisdiction is so forgiving. Don't forget to be sure you have properly headed your section on defenses, and you must use them or lose them. Read your local rules!

D. Counterclaims

It is perfectly possible for a plaintiff and a defendant to view the same occurrence completely differently. Each thinks the other is the bad guy, and each thinks the other owes him something. Did the farmer's cabbage get eaten by the neighbor's goat, as plaintiff contends, or is the neighbor correct that the farmer is just trying to extort money from him? If the defendant's view of the case includes a belief that he is entitled to relief, not the plaintiff, you as his counsel will draft counterclaims setting out the facts, the law and the relief you seek just as though you were drafting an initial complaint.

The counterclaims will therefore start with new numbered paragraphs, starting from "1," and will set out the facts upon which you will rely for your claims. It is allowable to refer to your earlier answers and to your affirmative defenses by saying you incorporate them by reference into your counterclaims, but doing so doesn't replace setting out the facts you need to allege your counterclaims.

So, for example, assume the plaintiff is suing your defendant client for selling him a plot of polluted property, and is seeking rescission of the land deal. So far, plaintiff has only paid half of the purchase price. Your client believes that the plaintiff is trying to wiggle out of the deal because the real estate market crashed. He wants the deal to be completed and the plaintiff to pay him the rest of what he owes.

Your counterclaim will begin like this:

Counterclaims

1. Defendant incorporates by reference here all of the averments of his answers and affirmative defenses set out above.
2. In 1985, plaintiff and defendant agreed in writing that plaintiff would buy defendant's land. In that agreement, plaintiff agreed to pay half of the purchase price during the first year

of his ownership and the other half during the second year.

3. The plaintiff has now owned the property for three years. The plaintiff paid the first half due under the agreement, but has failed, despite repeated demands, to pay the second half.

If you believe you need to recite more underlying facts than just the barebones I recite above, do so. And depending on procedural rules and custom, you may have to do so. You know I am going to say this—how you draft your counterclaims will be determined by your local rules and by local custom.

Like affirmative defenses, counterclaims may be lost by failure to plead them. For example, under New Jersey's entire controversy doctrine, certain counterclaims must be pleaded in response to the complaint or be waived. These are called "mandatory counterclaims." N.J.R. Civ. Pro. 4:7-1, and arise out of the prudential need to determine all facets

Does The Defendant Have Claims?

If the defendant has claims against the plaintiff, they are COUNTERCLAIMS.

If the defendant has claims against other defendants, they are CROSSCLAIMS.

If the defendant has claims against third parties who are not involved in the litigation yet, they are THIRD PARTY CLAIMS, also known as impleader.

of a single dispute at once. In the federal courts, Rule 13 requires that:

> (a)(1) In General.
>
> A pleading must state as a counterclaim any claim that—at the time of its service—the pleader has against an opposing party if the claim:
>
> (A) arises out of the transaction or occurrence that is the subject matter of the opposing party's claim; and
>
> (B) does not require adding another party over whom the court cannot acquire jurisdiction.

Once again, use it or lose it.

E. Cross-Claims

Many new lawyers get confused between counter and cross-claims. Cross-claims are claims you have against another defendant in the case. This defendant has been sued along with your client. Federal Rule 13 says:

> (g) Crossclaim Against a Coparty.
>
> A pleading may state as a crossclaim any claim by one party against a coparty if the claim arises out of the transaction or occurrence that is the subject matter of the original action or of a counterclaim, or if the claim relates to any property that is the subject matter of the original action. The crossclaim may include a claim that the coparty is or may be liable to the

crossclaimant for all or part of a claim asserted in the action against the crossclaimant.

The rules refers to coparties, as opposed to co-defendants, because sometimes there are multiple plaintiffs in a case and they have claims against each other that arise because of a defendant's answer or affirmative defenses or counterclaims.

Again, in certain jurisdictions, you must plead certain mandatory crossclaims or lose them forever. See, e.g., N.J.R. Civ. Pro. 4:7-5.

F. Third-Party Complaints

Your client may have been the only one sued, the only defendant in the case. Yet you or your client may know or believe that others are responsible for the damage claimed by the plaintiff—if not completely responsible, at least partially so. If the plaintiff won't sue those parties directly, you may have to bring them into the case by filing a third party complaint. All the same considerations go into drafting third party complaints that go into drafting original complaints. The only difference is that you will refer to your client as "defendant/third party plaintiff," and to the new defendants as "third party defendant."

When can you file a third party complaint? Check your rules! You probably have a defined amount of time to do it after you answer the complaint. Should you believe as discovery progresses that others need to be added as third party defendants, you will need to ask the court for permission (also known as "leave") to do so, via motion.

You should be aware that adding a defendant can have adverse consequences in terms of forum and jurisdiction. For example, if your case is in federal court pursuant to the diversity statute, 28 U.S.C. Section 1441, and you add a non-diverse party, you destroy subject matter jurisdiction. The court on its own, or a party by motion, may seek to have the case remanded to the state court pursuant to 28 U.S.C. Section 1447. Failure to remand to state court, or a failure to sever the case against the non-diverse party and have a parallel case in state court, will render the ensuing litigation a nullity for lack of subject matter jurisdiction.

Even where joining third parties to the suit does not destroy subject matter jurisdiction, the new parties may validly claim that the forum is inconvenient (forum non conveniens) or that venue is not proper. You should consider whether your client has the risk of losing the current forum by adding new parties, and if so, if it matters to the strength of your defense.

G. Removal

A state court defendant has the option to "remove" the case to federal court if there is diversity of citizenship between the plaintiff and the defendant. See 28 U.S.C. Sections 1441 and 1446. For strategic reasons, as I mentioned above, the defendant may wish to have the case heard in federal court, and so removal will be the option of choice. But there is no mandatory requirement that a case be removed just because there is complete diversity of citizenship; the defendant may wish to remain in state court.

Again, this is a decision that you must help your client make. Among your considerations will be whether the state court system is overly generous to plaintiffs, or whether the state court system tends to favor local defendants. In Philadelphia, the defense lawyers' mantra was to be in federal court at all costs, to avoid the largesse of Philadelphia juries to plaintiffs. Here is where the local knowledge of your fellow lawyers can help you plan the best course of action for your client.

H. Miscellaneous Considerations

I like the "belt and suspenders" approach to litigation. Some might call my approach obsessive. But to be a good lawyer, you must cover every possibility and avoid leaving loopholes for your adversaries to jump into. When you prepare your affirmative defenses, counterclaims, crossclaims and third party complaints, you must be sure that every claim or defense that your client has, or could have, is spelled out. That will mean, in many cases, that you are repeating yourself in defenses, counterclaims, crossclaims and third party complaints. As the comedian Jerry Seinfeld notably said, "not that there's anything wrong with that."

However, a claim against a third party can open a Pandora's box of problems. For example, F.R.C.P. 13 makes it clear that you must bring a claim or waive it, unless the party against whom you will be making the claim cannot be subjected to the court's jurisdiction. So what are you to do if your client has been sued in federal court under the diversity statute, 28 U.S.C. Section 1332, and she has a claim against a third party who is actually responsible for plaintiff's damages but whose presence would destroy diversity?

If your client brings in the new party, and doing so destroys diversity, the district court will have no further subject matter jurisdiction, and anything that occurs thereafter in the case is a nullity. Your client will have to bring the claim against the third party directly in state court. There will then be two separate actions pending that would require a judge, whether in the state or the federal court, to stay one of the actions. However, assuming that the defendant will not have a statute of limitations problem, he has the option of litigating his case against the third party at some later date, rather than in two parallel forums.

An example of a claim where there is no statute of limitations problem: a claim for indemnity. The indemnifying party—the indemnitor—promises that if the indemnified party—the indemnitee—is forced to pay a sum of money to another, the indemnitor will pay the debt, or repay the indemnitee. So assuming your client has a claim for indemnity against a third party, that claim does not actually arise until your client is forced to pay the plaintiff. The statute of limitations doesn't begin to run until there is a judgment in the underlying action. As the notes to N.J.R. Civ. Pro. 4:7-5 put it, "the cause of action for indemnity accrues when the event fixing liability occurs."

But beware! The rules in your jurisdiction may require that all claims, including indemnity claims, be brought in one action. New Jersey's entire controversy doctrine requires that a claim for indemnity against a party already in the litigation must be made in the main case or waived forever. N.J.R. Civ. Pro. 4:30A. If the indemnitor is not already in the case, however, the entire controversy doctrine doesn't require his presence, although the New Jersey rules as currently drafted require notice to all parties of the existence of the indemnitor and the nature of his role in the transaction or occurrence. Id. The doctrine in New Jersey has changed over the years, demonstrating that it is wise to check your rules before making a decision about adding parties or claims.

Please Judge, May I Have Attorneys' Fees?

As I mentioned above, when crafting a complaint, a plaintiff may be entitled to attorneys' fees if he prevails. This is usually a matter of statute, since under our common law we have the so-called "American rule," that each party bears its own legal costs, win or lose. Defendants, too, are entitled to their legal fees pursuant to the same statutes if they are the prevailing party. So be sure to add a request for attorneys' fees to your Wherefore clauses, whether in the answer, counterclaim, cross-claim or third party complaint.

Additionally, your jurisdiction may authorize the court to shift your fees to your opponent as a sanction, where the court finds that the plaintiff has abused the court system in some fashion. See, for example, F.R.C.P. 11(c)(4). Don't forget to ask for your client's fees.

Because I never want to be told by a court that I have brought my client's indemnity claim too late, I always add it in as an affirmative defense, a counterclaim (if appropriate) or a counterclaim or third party claim without waiting for the cause of action to accrue. If I'm in federal court and my client is looking for indemnity from a party whose presence would destroy diversity, and I don't want to lose my federal forum, I will initiate an action in state court against the indemnitor. That's what I mean by "belt and suspenders"—do everything to maximize your client's victory. Leave no stone unturned.

Going Through The Motions

You will have many opportunities during the course of litigating your client's case to draft motions and supporting briefs. The topic is overwhelming, and I will not attempt to discuss all the possible motions that are available to a defendant. I will discuss only those preliminary motions that you may decide to draft instead of answering the complaint. As I discussed above, a defendant may move to dismiss part or all of the complaint or to force the plaintiff to state its claim more fully.

Be aware that your motion may make sense to the plaintiff as well as to you, and that the plaintiff usually has the right to amend the complaint or to "replead." As I mentioned earlier, in federal court, Rule 15 provides that a party may amend its pleading once as a matter of course within twenty one days of serving the original or within twenty one days after service upon it of a responsive pleading or motion. So expect that your complaint to the court about the complaint will help the plaintiff cure the defect about which you are complaining. Check your rules to determine what options the plaintiff has to respond to your motion.

A. Find out The Nomenclature and The Requirements

Depending on the jurisdiction you're in, the document you file in order to assert the defects in the complaint may be called a motion (federal court, for example), a notice of motion (New Jersey state court, for example), a preliminary objection (as in Pennsylvania), or something else entirely. Again, read your rules for both the nomenclature and the requirements (Such as, do you need a cover sheet? A brief? Numbered paragraphs in the motion?).

There are three schools of thought about motions and briefs (and I am indebted to Spencer Punnett for pointing out the third). The first is the long-winded approach, which I believe is not as effective as the others. A lawyer using the long-winded approach sets out in the motion every point he makes in the brief, thereby duplicating unnecessarily his points and contributing to the killing of trees in service of the additional pages he files (except in those jurisdictions where filing is electronic). By contrast, my preferred method is to file a one-sentence motion, incorporating the brief by reference: "For the reasons stated in the attached memorandum of law, incorporated herein by reference, defendant moves to dismiss the complaint pursuant to F.R.C.P. 12(b)(6)." This gives the judge and/or the judge's clerk a heads up as to the point of the submission.

The third method, which is the middle approach, is described by Spencer this way: "Some state court judges wouldn't read anything on a motion until the start of the hearing on the motion. So I would always set out the basics in very simple form in the motion itself—usually no more than one page—along with an accompanying memo. That way, the judge could quickly get the gist just by reading the motion, sort of like an executive summary."

I can hear some of you saying: "Are you sure methods two and three are okay?" As a matter of style, they are better than okay. But do your local rules allow it? Does local practice support it? Always check the rules and local practice.

When I was a young and extremely inexperienced law clerk at a big firm, I made the mistake of reading the federal rules and not asking any questions. This led me to prepare a motion for summary judgment, as requested by a senior partner, with no supporting brief. (For some reason, every brief in every jurisdiction I've practiced in is called a "Memorandum of Law" whether or not it also discusses facts. Whatever you call it, you need one.) Don't do what I did.

Your rules will tell you what a brief should contain in your jurisdiction. For example, do you need a table of contents, or a table of authorities?

Must the motion be verified (i.e., sworn to)? Do your rules require a particular form of cover sheet? How do you prove that the motion was properly served (i.e., a certification of service)?

In addition to a brief, your motion should include a proposed form of order, showing the judge what you hope her ruling will look like.

Your rules will also tell you when to file and serve your brief. In some jurisdictions, the brief and the motion are not served together.

And in some jurisdictions, such as Pennsylvania, your motion to dismiss will actually be called something else. In Pennsylvania, the following motions to dismiss are called preliminary objections, and are considered pleadings, not motions: lack of subject matter jurisdiction, improper venue, lack of specificity, failure to state a claim legally or factually, lack of capacity to sue or non-joinder of a necessary party, misjoinder of a cause of action, pendency of another action, failure to exhaust administrative remedies and full, complete and adequate non-statutory remedy at law (i.e., the case has already been decided before in a different court and the plaintiff is seeking another bite of the apple). See Pa. R. Civ. Pro. 1028. Because they are pleadings, not motions, you will not file a separate memorandum of law with the preliminary objections you file; instead, you will include your legal arguments and your factual arguments together, in numbered paragraphs, in the preliminary objections document. Unless you are in a county with local rules that require a motion and brief to accompany the preliminary objections, such as Philadelphia county:

> (3) Within thirty (30) days after filing Preliminary Objections with the Prothonotary, provided an amended pleading has not been filed, the

> objecting party shall file a Motion to Determine the Preliminary Objections, together with the following:
> (a) a copy of the preliminary objections;
> (b) a Brief or Memorandum of Law, as set forth in Phila. Civ. R. * 210; and
> (c) copies of all items necessary or relevant to the disposition of the preliminary objections. This shall include the complaint, answer, and reply to new matter. All such items shall be included or attached and marked as exhibits separately. The Court may decide preliminary objections against a party who fails to attach to the filing those items sufficient to enable the Court to determine the preliminary objections.

Philadelphia Local Rule *1028. (The so-called "star" rules are the county local rules.)

Which only goes to show: read your rules. Every court is different. As I mentioned earlier, Louisiana is a civil code state, with causes of action different from the federal courts' and most state courts'. Nevertheless, even among the district courts and the state courts of the other 49 states, local peculiarities often harken back to the old days of common law pleading.

For example, in Pennsylvania, the clerk of the court is called the "Prothonotary," certain motions are called petitions, and the request for issuance of a writ or an order to show cause is called a "praecipe." Pennsylvania is not alone in its adherence to archaic terms. Michigan, for example, uses a "praecipe" to put a motion on the docket for disposition. The term is used in Ohio as well.

I cannot begin to set out all the differences in practice in each jurisdiction, but I hope that these examples will alert you to the necessity of referring to the rules and local practice, in order to do it right, the first time.

B. Strategize

As I mentioned earlier in this book, the decision you will make upon receiving the complaint, as the defendant's advocate, is strategic—do you answer the complaint, or do you instead respond? In some situations, such as where there is no subject matter jurisdiction, you must file a motion to dismiss or risk going through an entire litigation that is a nullity and trying to explain to your client why he has shelled out big bucks for you to try a case that shouldn't have been brought in the first place. But how about the "lesser" motions, the ones that rely on defects in the complaint that can be waived, such as improper venue? How do you decide whether or not to bring a motion to dismiss? Here are the factors I take into account when discussing with my client whether we should answer or move in response to the complaint:

1. What are the chances of success of a motion or motions?
2. What advantage does the defendant gain by filing the motion(s)?
3. How much will it cost?

Going in reverse order, let me first talk about cost. Many defendants are so infuriated that they have been sued that they tell you: cost be damned! I don't care how much it costs. I want you to make the plaintiff's life a living hell! However, after the first hefty bill from a law firm, defendants tend to calm down and spend less. The most important thing for you to do is to put in writing what you believe the costs will be for a motion, a response, an oral argument and the like, so that the defendant cannot turn on you, his advocate, when the bill arrives. Seeing the cost in black and white tends to focus the defendant's mind, and may determine the course of how you handle the defense.

I attach at the end of the book a template for a proposed litigation budget, that will help you think about what goes into a litigation in terms of both activities and cost.

Even where your client has a lot to gain and the importance of filing a motion is obvious, as where the motion is case dispositive—for example, where you are asking the court to dismiss for lack of subject matter jurisdiction—cost should be a factor in your decision-making. Filing a motion may be using a cannon where a small pistol will do. In other words, you may want to discuss the matter with plaintiff's counsel. By alerting her to the jurisdictional defect, you give her the opportunity to dismiss the case or cure the defect. Everyone saves on legal fees.

Of course, plaintiff's counsel may be unreasonable. She may not care that the court has no subject matter jurisdiction. She may say to you: tell it to the judge. In that case, you must file your motion. And, also, you must make sure that if your opponent consents to fix the problem, she does so well before you must file an answer or other response.

There is nothing worse than having an opponent string you along, saying she will dismiss the case, and then finding out the day before your answer is due that she will not. This violates the golden rule I mentioned above (do unto others, etc.), but some lawyers just don't seem to care. If necessary, while the plaintiff's lawyer is "thinking" about it, get her to sign a stipulation for an extension of time to answer or otherwise plead. And you, young lawyer—don't leave it to the last minute! Keep bugging your adversary, and if it looks as though she won't cooperate, draft and file your motion. Saving your client money is important, but not missing a deadline is even more important.

I have often heard the term "scorched earth litigation," as I'm sure you have. Jim McElhaney calls the practitioner who engages in such litigation "Mongo." Years ago, when the eponymous movies were popular, we called them "Rambo litigators." Whatever you call it, it doesn't serve your client, unless your client demands it and is willing to pay for it. Two cases in point: the case of the hateful plaintiff, and the case of the clueless counsel.

In the first case, the hateful plaintiff sued my client out of irrational hatred. My client irrationally hated the plaintiff right back. This defendant was willing to pay anything to make the plaintiff's life miserable. We filed motions, took depositions, and spent easily $100,000 in legal fees, all of which the client paid willingly. We wore the plaintiff down, and the plaintiff abandoned the effort. While I, the reasonable woman, would never be a Rambo or create scorched earth, my relentless pursuit of vindication for my client was successful and cost my client a lot of money.

In the second case, the clueless lawyer misnamed my defendant client and purported to serve the client by mailing me a copy of the complaint. In this case, my client wanted this case to go away, but didn't want to pay for unnecessary motions, such as a motion to dismiss for improper service. I knew that the plaintiff's counsel would eventually get the right name and figure out how to serve my client; we had seen the lawsuit coming. So rather than file a motion to dismiss, or simply ignore the complaint, I wrote the plaintiff's lawyer a letter, suggesting that she refile the complaint with the correct name. As a quid pro quo, I would accept service of the complaint as corrected on behalf of the client. (Of course, I discussed this with the defendant first, to ensure he approved.) Plaintiff's counsel agreed, and once the lawsuit was properly filed, I responded with—a motion to dismiss for failure to state a claim. We won. I knew I would have to file a motion eventually, I just didn't want to file one that could just as easily have been resolved with a letter or phone call. I saved my client money.

U.S. Magistrate Judge Morton Denlow, of the Northern District of Illinois, has put it succinctly: "Many of the issues raised by pretrial motions could be avoided if attorneys would use an antique piece of technology: the telephone." There are times when filing a motion is a must; there are times when the issues can be resolved through informal means. It pays you and your client to determine which it is in your case.

Now for the second factor: what will the defendant gain from filing a motion? As I have discussed above, the defendant who moves for a change of venue, or for dismissal or transfer based on forum non conveniens, or for removal from state court, may gain an advantage by successfully asking the court to change the locale of the trial to a forum where he is more likely to prevail. All of the defense witnesses may be based elsewhere, and a change of forum will allow the defendant to call as many of them as necessary without worrying about the cost of travel, or even whether or not the witnesses will travel in the first place. You can see the advantage to your client of finding a forum you favor.

Then there are defects, such as failure of service of process or lack of personal jurisdiction, that can be waived by the defendant. Is it worth fighting about, even if you prevail on a motion? According to Magistrate Judge Denlow, most judges will allow the plaintiff to correct these deficiencies, if they can be corrected; he views these motions as "largely a waste of time." However, failure of service can turn out to be a case dispositive issue, as in the case I talked about above, where a $13 million judgment was vacated because service on defendant corporation was not proper. In that situation, it certainly is a gain for the defendant to bring a motion to dismiss.

Moving to dismiss for failure to state a claim is in many ways the equivalent of a motion for summary judgment, although instead of relying on information gathered in discovery, as a summary judgment motion does, a failure to state a claim motion relies only on the pleadings. Under the federal rules, it is often referred to as a Rule 12(b)(6) motion. It is case dispositive, and therefore of great potential value to your client. However, because it is such a powerful motion, some judges and some jurisdictions tend to disfavor them, and will not grant them very often. I have heard a judge, explaining the civil procedural rules in one jurisdiction, explain that no lawyer should file a motion to dismiss for failure to state a claim in his court, because he doesn't grant them.

Additionally, unless you are sure it is a slam-dunk, you run the risk of losing and educating your opponent about your case when you file a 12(b)(6) type motion. To the extent the plaintiff can replead, or amend the complaint, a 12(b)(6) type motion gives the advantage to the plaintiff, not the defendant. The possible exception is where you successfully move to dismiss an amended complaint as well as the original complaint. In such a case, even where the court

Venue and Forum Non Conveniens

Assume that the plaintiff has laid the action where venue is proper, pursuant to statute or the rules of procedure. Also assume you, as the defendant's counsel, don't think the venue will be good for your client. Do you have any recourse? You do, under the doctrine of forum non conveniens. By invoking forum non conveniens, you can ask the court to dismiss the case or transfer it to a different court, on the grounds, for example, that defendant can't get a fair trial in the forum, or that all the witnesses are elsewhere. In other words, the doctrine presumes venue is correct, and yet allows a party to assert that the forum is unfair.

grants the plaintiff leave to amend again, the plaintiff may be so disheartened that he is willing to settle favorably—or even to give up.

Which leads me to the most important factor for your consideration: what are your chances of success with your motion? In my experience, judges do not often grant case dispositive motions, unless the reason is lack of subject matter jurisdiction. The judge who told us lawyers not to bother filing a 12(b)(6) type motion in his court was not revealing a state secret.

Will the U. S. Supreme Court's rulings on heightened pleading standards in Bell Atlantic v. Twombly and Ashcroft v. Iqbal result in more judges granting 12(b)(6) type motions? Time will tell. As the caselaw develops, however, your client may not want to be on the cutting edge of new law if there is a great risk of failure in his particular case.

Ethical Considerations

Whether you are drafting a pleading or a motion, you have an ethical duty to play fair. Most jurisdictions have the equivalent of Rule 11 of the federal rules, requiring the attorney to certify that the pleading or motion is well-grounded in fact and law. See, for example, Texas Rule of Civil Procedure 10.001:

> § 10.001. SIGNING OF PLEADINGS AND MOTIONS. The signing of a pleading or motion as required by the Texas Rules of Civil Procedure constitutes a certificate by the signatory that to the signatory's best

knowledge, information, and belief, formed after reasonable inquiry:

(1) the pleading or motion is not being presented for any improper purpose, including to harass or to cause unnecessary delay or needless increase in the cost of litigation;
(2) each claim, defense, or other legal contention in the pleading or motion is warranted by existing law or by a nonfrivolous argument for the extension, modification, or reversal of existing law or the establishment of new law;
(3) each allegation or other factual contention in the pleading or motion has evidentiary support or, for a specifically identified allegation or factual contention, is likely to have evidentiary support after a reasonable opportunity for further investigation or discovery; and
(4) each denial in the pleading or motion of a factual contention is warranted on the evidence or, for a specifically identified denial, is reasonably based on a lack of information or belief.

C. Drafting A Brief

I love to write. And drafting a memorandum of law, or brief, is almost as good as writing a short story. Why? Because a good brief gives me the latitude I need to tell my client's story persuasively, without having to insert "magic language" or paragraph numbering or incorporations by reference. It is easier to persuade in a brief than in a complaint or an answer. When it comes to "dry" versus "wet" communication, a brief is the ultimate legal form for telling an interesting story.

I'm sure you're tired of me saying this, but the first thing to do when preparing a brief is to read your rules. Many jurisdictions prescribe in the civil rules what a brief should contain. In general, though, briefs follow certain historical forms.

First, you will have an "Introduction," explaining the relief your client wants and the reasons she's entitled to that relief. Then you will have a section entitled "Undisputed Facts," or just "Facts," or "Plaintiff's Allegations," or "Statement of the Case," depending on local practice. You will tell the story your way, accepting as true the facts set out in the complaint, since for a 12(b) type motion, you must assume the allegations are true; your argument is that even if the facts alleged are true, the complaint should be dismissed. Then you will have a section on "The Law," or "Argument." Here you will set out all the relevant legal propositions that support your case, and of course cite the cases that support your position. Finally, a section entitled "Conclusion" will say: "For all the foregoing reasons, plaintiff's complaint should be dismissed with prejudice."

Of course, if you are the plaintiff's counsel and you receive a motion and brief, you will have to respond to it. You have two choices: amend the complaint to remove the defendant's objections, if you can; or oppose the motion by drafting a brief. Be sure to file your opposition or your amended complaint in a timely fashion.

For many lawyers, drafting a brief is the height of lawyering. I say this because there are fewer and fewer trials all the time, and most litigators spend their time on paper and not in the courtroom. Occasionally, you may even get to argue your motion orally, but the writing of a persuasive brief is the ultimate manifestation of the passion lawyers have for their clients' position. Enjoy it. And make it great.

Conclusion

In this short discussion, I have tried to raise the many complex issues that arise at the beginning of a litigation so you will be aware of them. Please don't consider this to be the final word on any of the issues.

The most important guiding principle for you should be the best interests of your client. The goal, unless your client instructs you to the contrary, is to advance the ball in a cost-effective manner.

Even if your client wants you to do the whole scorched earth thing, you cannot do it unless it is ethically permissible. Pleadings interposed solely for the purpose of delay, or for the purpose of harassment, should and probably will be stricken. Worse, they could subject you personally to sanctions, and possibly even to disbarment. If your client wants you to do something your gut tells you is wrong, don't do it. And if your gut is not a reliable indicator of appropriate behavior, find yourself an ethics mentor to counsel you.

Once you get your first few pleadings and motions under your belt, you will be better able to see how the many interlocking concepts fit together. And when you do, be sure to help out some other newbie who is dazed and confused, just as you used to be.

Checklists and Litigation Budget

Checklist for Drafting A Complaint

1. Talk to your client.
2. Be sure you understand the facts, the issues, and what your client wants.
3. Investigate the facts.
4. Investigate the applicable law, including the statute of limitations.
5. Determine the causes of action available, and the elements of each cause.
6. Determine the remedies available to your client.
7. Choose a forum to sue in.
8. Be sure you have the right venue.
9. Be sure you can obtain personal jurisdiction over the defendant.
10. Be sure the defendant can be served.
11. Be sure your chosen forum has subject matter jurisdiction.
12. Determine if the complaint must be verified (sworn to).
13. Ask for a jury trial if you want it.
14. Determine the filing fee and any other local requirements for filing the complaint, such as cover sheets.

Checklist for Drafting A Response

1. Talk to your client.
2. Review the complaint and be sure you know what your deadline for response is.
3. Investigate the facts.
4. Research the law upon which plaintiff relies.
5. Determine your defenses, factual and legal.
6. Decide whether it is more advantageous to answer the complaint or to file a motion.
7. Determine if the forum court is adverse to your client or his defenses, and if you should try to move the matter.
8. Read the rules in your jurisdiction on defenses and denials, and determine how the defenses, denials and facts left out of the complaint should be presented in your answer. (Should they be labeled new matter? Affirmative defenses?)
9. Determine if your client has claims against others arising out of the facts set forth in the complaint, including indemnity claims, whether the claims are against the plaintiff, co-defendants, or others not yet parties.
10. Ensure that you have included every possible defense to the claims that your client has.
11. Ensure that you have included every possible claim against others that your client has.
12. Determine whether or not there is a filing fee in your jurisdiction for answers, or for other responses, and whether or not there are other requirements specific to your jurisdiction for filing an answer or a motion.
13. Be sure you properly serve the answer or other response.

Litigation Budget Template

Case Name: ______________________________

Court: ___________________________________

Docket No.: ______________________________

TASK	HOURS REQUIRED TO COMPLETE TASK (broken down by attorneys/paralegals providing services)	HOURLY RATES OF ATTORNEYS/ PARALEGALS	TOTAL FEES
A. Initial Review and Pleadings			
B. Factual Investigation & Initial Evaluation			
C. Written Discovery Propounded by			
1. Client			
2. Other Litigants			
D. Depositions			
1. Expert(s)			
a. Defend			
b. Take			
c. Sit in			
2. Lay Witness(s)			
a. Defend			
b. Take			
c. Sit in			
E. Discovery Motions			
F. Legal Research			
G. Settlement/ADR			
H. Non-Discovery Motions & Briefs			
I. Trial Briefs			
J. Trial Preparation			
K. Conduct of Trial			
L. Post-Trial Matters			

TOTAL FEES

EXPENSES	Amount
A. Consultants/Experts	
1.	
2.	
3.	
4.	
B. Travel	
1. Air	
2. Lodging	
3. Meals	
4. Car Rental/Taxi	
5. Other	
C. Copying/Microfilm	
D. Communications/Phone/Fax	
E. Computer Research	
F. Delivery/Fed EX/Messenger	
G. Document Management	
H. Transcript/Reporter	
I. Miscellaneous	

Total Fees and Expenses:

Index

About the Author

Janet S. Kole has been practicing law for thirty years, and is now mostly retired and writing about the law. She is the author of Chasing Paper (ABA), and co-author of Post Mortem (Doubleday), and is the editor of Environmental Litigation (ABA). She lives in Philadelphia, PA, rural Maryland, and Florida.

She is passionate about the law, her clients, and boats. And about her family, Gabe Steerman and Wendy Leebov, and Nikki and Chaim Bank and the grandkids. And she likes golf a lot. And writing.